CW00644360

THE SCOTTISH COVENANTERS

The
Scottish
Covenanters

Their Origins, History and Distinctive Doctrines

Johannes G. Vos.

Blue Banner Productions

BLUE BANNER PRODUCTIONS
James A. Dickson Books, 12 Forrest Road,
Edinburgh, EHI 2QN   Scotland.

First published 1940,
reprinted 1980,
by Board of Education and Publication of the Reformed
Presbyterian Church of North America.

This edition is re-set and reprinted with permission of
'Crown and Covenant Publications (Reformed Presbyterian
Church of North America)' 1998.

ISBN 0 9511484 4 3

Printed by Icon Press Ltd
Edinburgh

PREFACE

This book was written as a thesis and offered in partial fulfillment of the requirements for the graduate certificate of Westminster Theological Seminary in 1938. In the preparation of the material for publication a number of changes have been made.

Erastianism, against which the seventeenth century Covenanters contended so earnestly, is very much alive in the world today. In many lands the State is assuming control over larger and larger sections of human life, with the result that the independence and intrinsic powers of the Christian Church are being challenged by the conception of the unlimited functions and authority of the State. The fundamental distinction between the things of God and the things of Caesar is being questioned, and it is demanded of Christians that they render to Caesar not merely the things of Caesar, but the things of God as well. Real religious liberty is passing away, and the counterfeit, Erastian toleration, is taking its place. In the face of the present situation, the history of the Scottish Covenanters is both illuminating and encouraging. The author hopes that the present volume will help to show the true independence and autonomy of the Christian Church as over against the encroaching demands of the State, and also that it will help to convince Christian people of the sinfulness of compromise with Erastianism in any form whatever.

The author believes that the great principles for which the Scottish Covenanters contended are Scriptural and therefor valid for all time, though of course the application of the principles must vary according to the circumstances of different countries and periods of time. The foregoing statement does not mean, however, that the author accepts as

Scriptural everything for which the Covenanters contended. They were human and undoubtedly erred in some matters. For example Article II of the Solemn League and Covenant which pledges the covenanting parties to endeavor the "extirpation" of heresy and schism, can hardly be defended as Scriptural, unless by "extirpation" we understand some thing quite different from what the seventeenth century Covenanters seem to have meant by this term.

The sincere thanks of the author are due to Professor Paul Woolley of Westminster Theological Seminary for his helpful criticism of the thesis and valuable suggestions.

JOHANNES G. VOS
September 1, 1939

Postscript—40 Years Later.

*The conclusion of this book as it appeared in 1940 was an emphasis on the Scottish Covenanters' basic principle—**Jus Divinum**—"Divine Right" or "the Rights of God." (page 230) The by-passing of God which the Covenanters of Scotland witnessed against is far exceeded by the modern secular humanism of America. On every hand it is assumed that "Religion" is a private luxury of some people, having nothing to do with life. The First Amendment to the U.S. Constitution (adopted 1791) provides that "Congress shall make no law respecting an establishment of religion...," thus guarding against an official State Church. Today legislation, court decisions and public opinion hold that this statement means that there can be no connection between the government (and what may be connected with it), on the one hand, and "religion" on the other hand.*

God is placed on a reservation, and education,

culture, law, politics and life in general, are to proceed as if there were no God. In the face of this situation, the God-centered faith of the Covenanters is desperately needed. God is not dead, but His terrible judgment hangs over a nation that treats Him as an irrelevant private matter.

JOHANNES G. VOS
November 1, 1980

CONTENTS

	Page
Preface	5
Introduction	13

PART I. THE ORIGINS OF THE COVENANTERS 17

CHAPTER I. The Background of the Covenanting Movement: An Outline of the First Reformation in Scotland. 1560-1567 — 17

1. Antecedents of the Reformation... .. .. — 17
2. John Knox, the leader of the Reformation... .. — 19
3. The Legal Abolition of Roman Catholicism . .. — 23
4. The Character of the Reformed Church of Scotland .... — 25
5. The Relation between Church and State 1560-1567 .. .. — 26

CHAPTER II. Struggles Between Presbytery and Prelacy. 1567-1637 .. .. — 28

1. Introduction of Tulchan Bishops, 1572 .. ... — 28
2. Andrew Melville Leader against Prelacy.. .. — 29
3. Anti-Prelatic Actions of the General Assembly .. — 31
4. The Great Charter of Presbytery, 1592 .. .. — 32
5. Introduction of "Perpetual Moderators", 1607... — 34
6. Introduction of Complete Episcopacy, 1612 .... — 36
7. The Five Articles of Perth, 1618 .. .. — 38

8. The Controversy about the Book of Canons, 1636 39
9. The Controversy about the Liturgy, 1637 41

CHAPTER III. The Period of the Second Reformation. 1637-1651 45

1. The "Four Tables", 1637 45
2. The National Covenant of Scotland, 1638 46
3. Royal Opposition to Ecclesiastical Reform, 1638 49
4. The General Assembly of 1638 51
5. Continued Royal Opposition to Reform 53
6. The Solemn League and Covenant, 1643.. 55
7. The Westminster Assembly, 1643-1649 58
8. The Engagement, 1648 61
9. The Act of Classes, 1649 63
10. Negotiations with Charles II, 1650 64

CHAPTER IV. The Church of Scotland under the Commonwealth, 1651-1660 ... 66

1. Scotland Subjected to the Commonwealth, 1650-1652 66
2. The Controversy between Resolutioners and Protestors 68
3. Cromwell Suppresses the General Assembly, 1653 71
4. The State of the Church of Scotland under the Commonwealth 72
5. The Later Covenanters' Estimate of Cromwell .. 73
6. The Restoration of Charles II, 1660 75

PART II **THE HISTORY OF THE COVENANTERS**   77

CHAPTER I. The Period of Persecution.
1660-1688   77

1. Legal Enactments Affecting the Church of
   Scotland   77
2. The Ejection of Ministers, 1662   84
3. Covenanting Conventicles and the Proclamations Issued Against Them   86
4. The Indulgences and the Covenanters' Attitude
   Toward Them   91
5. The Covenanters' Attempts at Armed Resistance 101
6. Public Protests and Testimonies Issued by the
   Covenanters   106
7. The Precise Nature of the Covenanters' Claims
   During the Period of Persecution   122
8. Divisions Among the Covenanters During the
   Period of Persecution   129
9. The Extent of the Persecution Suffered by the
   Covenanters   133
10. The Condition of the Covenanters on the Eve
   of the Revolution   134

CHAPTER II. The Revolution Settlement.
1688-1690   138

1. The Revolution of 1688   138
2. The Legal Settlement of the Church of
   Scotland   139

3. The Attitude of the Covenanters to the Revolution Settlement   143
4. The Covenanters' Grounds for Dissent from the Revolution Settlement   147

CHAPTER III. The Reformed Presbyterians Since the Revolution   159

1. The Accession of John Macmillan to the Covenanting Societies   159
2. The Organization of the Reformed Presbytery, 1743   165
3. The Division of the Reformed Presbytery, 1753   170
4. The Division of the Reformed Presbyterian Synod, 1863   176
5. The Union of the Larger Reformed Presbyterian Synod with the Free Church, 1876   178

PART III.   **THE DISTINCTIVE DOCTRINES OF THE COVENANTERS ..**   184

CHAPTER I.   The Continuing Obligation of the Scottish Covenants   184

1. The Origin of Covenanting at the First Reformation   184
2. Analysis of the Covenants of 1580, 1638 and 1643   186
3. Do the Covenants Purport to be Perpetually Binding?   193
4. The Perpetual Obligation of the Covenants as Held by the Early Covenanters   194
5. The Perpetual Obligation of the Covenants the Formal Principle of the Covenanting

Movement   202

CHAPTER II.   The Sole Headship of Christ
                   Over the Church   207

   1.   The Anti-Erastian Character of the Coven-
       anting Movement   207
   2.   The Covenanters not Opposed to the
       Principle of Establishment   210
   3.   The Effectiveness of the Covenanters'
       Testimony for the Sole Headship of Christ
       over the Church   212

CHAPTER III. The Covenanters' Doctrine of
                   Christian Civil Government..   ..   214

   1.   The Mediatorial Kingship of Christ over
       the Nations   214
   2.   Scripture the Rule for the Regulation of
       Civil Affairs   223
   3.   The Uniqueness of the Reformed Presbyterian
       Doctrine of Christian Civil Government   225

       BIBLIOGRAPHY   227

INTRODUCTION

In Scotland, probably more fully than in any other country in Christendom, the conception of the Church as a witnessing body has been developed. Questions of truth and error are not settled by majority votes, and it has happened more than once in the history of the Christian Church that principles maintained by a small and despised minority have later been accepted as sound and Scriptural by large sections of the Church, or even, as in the case of the truth for which Athanasius contended, by the whole Church.

In no portion of Scottish Church history is the conception of the Church as a witnessing organ more prominent than in the Covenanting and Reformed Presbyterian movement. It is the very essence of the Covenanters' conception of witness bearing that testimony must be borne in the face of opposition, without respect of persons and regardless of consequences. Even those who regard the Covenanters as having been in error cannot fail to see something heroic in Cameron disowning the house of Stuart at Sanquhar, Cargill solemnly excommunicating Charles II at the Torwood, and Renwick awaiting execution refusing to yield so much as a hair's breadth of his principles, even to save his life. Such men scorned compromise, and counted not their lives dear unto themselves. They were at the opposite pole from the Church politicians of their day who could bargain or compromise for the sake of present advantage. Like Abraham when he was about to sacrifice Isaac, the true Covenanters did not hesitate to do what they knew to be right, even though it might seem to be utterly inexpedient, even to the extent of cutting off witnesses for the truth from the land. Like Luther, they believed that it is neither safe nor right to act against conscience. Their philosophy was that "one with God is a majority", and from the sentences of both Church and State they appealed to a higher tribunal, the judgment-seat of the all-just God who does according to his own will in the army of heaven, and among the inhabitants of the earth. The mills of God may grind slowly, but they grind exceeding small, and men with the convictions of the Covenanters could afford to wait for their vindication, confident that God would plead his own cause and vindicate his servants, not only at the Last Great Day, but in a lesser way during the historical process itself. For the Covenanters were not contending and suffering in any merely human conflict; their whole philosophy was theocentric and theocratic, and their aim was to witness for the truth of God, to engage in the Lord's controversy and to fight the Lord's battles in spite of any human opposition whatever. As Cargill said, they would get God glorified on earth, and that was more than a mere entrance into heaven.

Of the Postmillenialism which is so common among Reformed Presbyterians today there appears scarcely a trace in the sermons, testimonies and other documents of the Covenanters until comparatively recent times. The notion that the "kingdom conception" of modern religious liberalism is substantially the same as the doctrine of the kingship of Christ over the nations for which the historical Covenanters contended is utterly at variance with the facts. The modern semi-rationalistic evolutionistic idea that the Kingdom of God is to come by the gradual accomplishment of various humanitarian social reforms and the gradual leavening of human society with Christian (or pseudo-Christian) ethical principles, apart from the supernatural regeneration and conversion to Christ of the mass of individuals making up that society, is utterly foreign to the theology of the historical Covenanters, as it is to the Westminster Standards which they held. They were supernaturalists, and far too consistent to believe that society as a whole could be transformed by the so-called social gospel until the mass of individuals composing that society had first been individually transformed by the grace of God and had become Christian believers in the evangelical sense. The Kingdom of God in which they believed was not one that could be attained by a society which rejects the whole supernatural system and basis of Christianity, while attempting to put in practice part of the ethical principles of Christianity not for the glory of the sovereign God but for the benefit of human society. The historical Covenanters held the theology, including the eschatology, of the Westminster Standards, and any modern developments which are out of harmony with the theology of the Westminster Standards are therefore at variance with the views held by the Covenanters throughout their history.

It remains to be stated that pacifism, which has been accepted by some Reformed Presbyterians in recent years, is utterly incompatible, not only with the actual words of the Westminster Standards, but also with the historic position of the Covenanters as well as with their actions during the period of persecution. Unlike the Quakers, the Covenanters always held that it is lawful to wage war in defence of liberty, religion and life. They believed that self-defence is the inalienable right of every righteous man. They condemned the doctrine that the reformation of either the Church or the State must be effected by the sword, but they always held to the legitimacy of defensive warfare. If the principle of pacifism, as held by some modern Reformed Presbyterians, is a sound and Scriptural one, then Cameron should not have resisted the king's troops at Ayrsmoss, the armed conventicles were sinful assemblies, and the Covenanters in the "killing time" should have submitted to being slaughtered without even an attempt at organized self-defence.

Finally, the Covenanters never were schismatic or sectarians. They never seceded from the Church of Scotland; they simply elected to remain independent of that body as it was reorganized at the Revolution Settlement. Though in fact the Reformed Presbyterian Church is one denomination among many today, Reformed Presbyterians have always been opposed to denominationalism and have regarded divisions in the body of Christ as inherently sinful. They would have the visible Church to be one, but not at the price of doctrinal indifferentism or compromise with error. Their claim is to be the legitimate continuation and spiritual succession of the Church of Scotland as it was in the period of the Second Reformation. And with the validity of the positions taken by the Church of Scotland at the Second Reformation, the validity of the claims of the Covenanters must stand or fall.

PART I

THE ORIGINS OF THE COVENANTERS

CHAPTER I

THE BACKGROUND OF THE COVENANTING MOVEMENT: AN OUTLINE OF THE FIRST REFORMATION IN SCOTLAND, 1560-1567

1. Antecedents of the Reformation.

The Church of Rome held control of the religious life of Scotland for a comparatively short period. Scotland early received Christianity in its Celtic, non-Roman form. It was not until the time of Queen Margaret, in the latter part of the eleventh century, that Celtic Christianity finally gave way to Roman Catholicism. From that time until the middle of the sixteenth century Scotland was a land of dense spiritual darkness, a land of many priests but very few witnesses for Jesus Christ, a land of many Churches but very little gospel.

Soon after the dawn of the Reformation in Germany, the doctrines of Protestantism began to reach Scotland. Probably the first Protestant witness in Scotland was Patrick Hamilton, a youth of noble lineage who had visited Luther in Germany in 1526. Hamilton hastened to return to Scotland that he might proclaim the good tidings there. It was not long until the Catholic clergy became aware of Hamilton's activities and determined to take action against him. In this movement James Beaton, Archbishop of St. Andrews, took the lead. Hamilton was condemned to death and burned at the stake on February 28, 1528, the first martyr of the Protestant Reformation in Scotland. Before going to his death he gave his outer garments to his servant, saying "This stuff will not help me in the fire, and will profit thee. After this you can receive from me no more good, but the example of my death, which, I pray thee, keep in mind; for, albeit it be bitter to the flesh, and fearful in man's judgment, yet it is the entrance into eternal life, which none shall possess that denies Christ Jesus before this wicked generation".[1]   After Hamilton's death, the news of this cruel deed spread rapidly, and some one warned Beaton that if he intended to burn any more, he should do it in cellars, "for the reek of Mr. Patrick Hamilton hath infected as many as it blew upon".[2]

In 1534 Beaton and his accomplices succeeded in obtaining the condemnation and execution by burning of three more Protestant witnesses, Norman Gourley, David Straiton and Henry Forest.[3] In 1538 five Protestants were burned in one fire at Edinburgh, four of them being former Roman Catholic ecclesiastics.[4] In the same year two Protestants, one of whom had been a friar, were burned at Glasgow.[5] James Beaton persecuted the Protestants as long as he could, but he was soon called to give an account of his deeds, for he died in 1539. His nephew, David Beaton, had served the Pope well in negotiating a marriage between King James of Scotland and Mary of Guise, and the Pope rewarded him by making him a Cardinal. Upon the death of James Beaton in

---

[1] Hetherington, W.M., *History of the Church of Scotland*, p. 37.

[2] *Ibid.*, p. 34.

[3] *Ibid.*, p. 38.

[4] *Ibid.*, p. 39.

[5] *Ibid.*

1539, David Beaton was made Archbishop of St. Andrews.[6]

In 1543 Cardinal Beaton procured the condemnation for heresy of five men and one woman, at Perth. The men were hanged and the woman drowned.[7] After this others were persecuted and some put to death in various places in Scotland.[8]

In 1546 another notable martyrdom, that of George Wishart, took place. Wishart had ventured to teach the Greek language in Scotland, which displeased the Bishop of Brechin. Wishart was called to answer for his deeds, but went to England, after which he was excommunicated and outlawed. He resided for a time at the University of Cambridge. In 1544 Wishart returned to Scotland and began to preach Protestant doctrines. Cardinal Beaton soon learned of this and instituted process against him. Wishart was accused of heresy listed under eighteen heads, all of which he answered with Scripture proofs, but in spite of this he was unanimously condemned by the Catholic clergy and sentenced to be executed by burning the following day. Cardinal Beaton sat in a window seat to observe the sufferings of the martyr.[9] In spite of these persecutions, perhaps even because of them, Protestantism continued to spread in Scotland and the day was hastening when Scotland would throw off the spiritual tyranny of the Church of Rome.

2. John Knox, the Leader of the Reformation.

At the time of the martyrdom of George Wishart, John Knox had been attending Wishart and wearing a sword

---

[6] *Ibid.*, p. 40.

[7] *Ibid.*, p. 43.

[8] *Ibid.*, p. 44.

[9] *Ibid.*, pp. 44-48.

in his defence. Knox wished to accompany Wishart to his trial, but Wishart refused to permit him to do so, saying, "Go back to your pupils; one is sufficient for one sacrifice".[10]

In the spring of 1547, a party of Protestant noblemen and gentlemen took the castle of St. Andrews and intrenched themselves in it as a protection from the power of the Catholic clergy. Early in April of that year, Knox entered the castle, influenced, no doubt, by sympathy toward those in the castle as well as by prudence which caused him to seek to escape the hostility of the hierarchy. Soon after Knox's arrival those gathered there gave him a solemn call to be their minister. As Calvin when importuned by Farel to remain and help in the work at Geneva was reluctant to comply, so Knox was overwhelmed with the thought of the responsibility involved in such a call, yet he did not dare refuse, and so he entered upon his work as a minister of the Gospel of Jesus Christ. It was not long before Knox made a bold attack on the Church of Rome. Before this, much of the controversy between Catholicism and Protestantism had been about details such as forms and ceremonies. Knox went the heart of the matter and boldly proclaimed that the Church of Rome was no true Church, but Antichrist. He would allow no appeal to any standard but the Word of God, and proposed nothing less than the entire reconstruction of the whole doctrinal and ecclesiastical system of Scotland on the basis of Scripture and of Scripture only.[11]

The Catholic party obtained help from France and attacked the castle of St. Andrews by land and by sea, and forced its surrender on July 31, 1547. According to the terms of the surrender, the defenders of the castle were guaranteed

---

[10] *Ibid.*, p. 45.

[11] *Ibid.*, p. 52.

their lives and liberty, but after the surrender of the castle, these terms were violated by the Catholics, and the prisoners, Knox among them, were sent to France and there compelled to serve as galley slaves. When Knox was finally released, he went to England, where he was offered the position of Bishop of Rochester. This, however, he refused, and he went to the Continent, and for a time ministered to a Protestant Church at Frankfurt; later he went to Geneva, and remained there until 1555 when he returned to Scotland.[12]

After his return to Scotland, Knox again took up his work of reformation. He sought out members of the nobility known to be favorable to Protestantism and conferred with them. Soon the Catholic clergy attacked him, and he was summoned to appear before them at Edinburgh on May 15th, 1556. When the day came, Knox appeared, but well supported by his numerous friends; the Catholic clergy were alarmed, and so no trial was held. Knox took advantage of the opportunity to preach the gospel publicly at Edinburgh. In July, 1556, he returned to Geneva.[13]   On May 2, 1559, Knox returned to Scotland for the last time. We may be sure that the Catholic clergy did not rejoice at his return. There is a tradition, which is probably not authentic, that a Catholic council which was about to try a number of Protestants dispersed on hearing the news of Knox's arrival in Scotland.[14]   On the 16th of June Knox preached at St. Andrews although he was aware of a plot to assassinate him there. To those who were fearful for his safety he said, "As for the fear of danger that may come to me, let no man be so solicitous; for my life is in the custody of him whose glory I seek. I desire the hand and weapon of no man to defend me. I only crave audience; which, if it be denied here unto me at

---

[12] *Ibid.*, p. 53.

[13] *Ibid.*, pp. 55-56.

[14] *Ibid.*, p. 67.

this time, I must seek further where I may have it".[15]   For four days Knox preached at St. Andrews against Popery, and so convincing were his words that the magistrates and people of the place determined to set up Protestant worship in the town, and at once removed the images and pictures from the Church, and destroyed the monasteries. The Archbishop of St. Andrews rushed to the Queen-regent with this news.[16]

Everything that is known of Knox shows that he was both a fearless man and a hater of compromise. When the General Assembly convened in 1561, Maitland of Lethington objected to the meeting, arguing that it was illegal to hold such a meeting without the Queen's consent. Knox replied, "Take from us the liberty of assemblies, and take from us the gospel. If the liberty of the Church must depend upon her allowance or disallowance, we shall want not only assemblies, but the preaching of the gospel".[17]   These words spoken by Knox at that early date, show his strong opposition to Erastian control of the Church by the State. Much of the later history of the Church of Scotland was a struggle to obtain and maintain the liberty claimed by Knox as an inherent right of the Church.

In 1563 Knox outspokenly denounced the idea that the Queen of Scotland should be permitted by the nobility to marry a Catholic. Knox was summoned to appear before the Queen in Council, and an argument took place between him and the Queen. Queen Mary tried threatening and also tears but Knox was unmoved by both, and stood his ground with great courage. At this time the nobility persuaded the Queen not to prosecute Knox. Later Knox was tried by a special

[15] *Ibid.*, p. 71.

[16] *Ibid.*, p. 72.

[17] *Ibid.*, p. 100.

court because of a letter which he had written and which was alleged to be treasonable; at the trial Knox defended himself ably. The principal charges were that he had illegally convoked the Queen's lieges and that he had charged the Queen with cruelty. After the hearing of the case Knox was ordered to retire until the next day, while the tribunal voted on the matter. He was acquitted by a large majority, and this acquittal was a great victory for the cause of the Reformation in Scotland.[18]

John Knox died on November 24th, 1572, and his funeral was held on the 26th. As the body was lowered into the grave, Morton, the Regent, looked into the open grave and said, "There lies he who never feared the face man".[19] Knox was a great man, a great patriot, and a great Christian.

3.   The legal abolition of Roman Catholicism.

The first legal enactment looking toward the Reformation in Scotland took place in 1542, when the Scottish Parliament, on the recommendation of Robert, Lord Maxwell, enacted over the protest of the Catholic clergy, that "it is lawful for the lieges to read the Bible in the vulgar tongue.[20] This act did not make it lawful to read the Bible in the vulgar tongue, in the sense of conferring a privilege which the State may confer or withhold; it simply recognized a right already existing, and thus made it impossible for the Catholic hierarchy to prosecute any person for simply reading a vernacular version of the Bible.

The Scottish Parliament met August 8 to 27, 1560 and

---

[18] *Ibid.*, pp. 105-107.

[19] *Ibid.*, p. 131.

[20] *Testimony of the Reformed Presbyterian Church of Ireland*, Part II, pp. 37-38.

took up the legal part of the work of Reformation in earnest. At the request of this Parliament, the Scots Confession of Faith was prepared by "the six Johns": Knox, Spottiswoode, Willock, Row, Douglas and Winram. This remarkable document was drawn up in four days, while the Parliament was in session, and contains a preface, twenty-five articles, and a conclusion. It is a good statement of Reformed doctrine, though of course not as complete and precise as the later Reformed confessions. The Confession was ratified by Parliament, 1560,[21] and continued to be the recognized doctrinal standard of the Church of Scotland for more than eighty years, until the Westminster Confession of Faith was adopted in 1647.

The same Parliament on August 24th adopted an "Act for abolishing the Pope and his usurped authority in Scotland" and an "Act against the Mass and the Sayers and Hearers Thereof",[22] and also an act repealing all former Acts of Parliament contrary to the Word of God, that is, all former pro-Catholic and anti-Protestant legislation.[23] This body of legislation was then sent to France for the approval of the King and Queen; this, however, was refused. The Protestants in Scotland held the acts to be valid without the royal consent.[24] This legislation abolished Roman Catholicism in Scotland and cleared the way for the Reformation.

The next important legislation affecting the Reformation was enacted in 1567. On April 19th Parliament passed an act securing to Protestant subjects immunity from

---

[21] Johnston, John C., *Treasury of the Scottish Covenant*, p.29.

[22] *Ibid.*, p. 31.

[23] Hetherington, *op. cit.*, pp. 82-83.

[24] *Ibid.*

civil injury.[25] On December 15th, Parliament ratified all the acts which had been passed in 1560 against Catholicism and in favor of the Reformation. Now legislation was enacted providing that in time to come no prince should be admitted to authority in Scotland without taking an oath to maintain the Protestant religion, and that all offices except those that were hereditary or were held for life, could be held by Protestants only.[26] The Reformation thus affected not only the Church but the State as well. It was purposed not only that the Church of Scotland should be a Reformed Church, but that the nation should be a Reformed nation.

4.   The Character of the Reformed Church of Scotland, 1560—1567.

The first General Assembly of the Church of Scotland was constituted at Edinburgh, December 20, 1560. The Assembly consisted of forty-two members, of whom only six were ministers.[27] At that time there were but twelve Protestant ministers in all Scotland.[28] The Assembly met by its own inherent authority, based on Scripture, and without any warrant or permission from the civil magistrate. During the following twenty years no less than forty Assemblies met without the presence of a commissioner appointed to represent the sovereign.[29]

An important act of the First General Assembly was the adoption of the First Book of Discipline. This document was prepared by "the six Johns" who had prepared the Scots Confession of Faith for the Parliament. The First Book of

---

[25] Johnston, *op. cit.*, p.39.

[26] Hetherington, *op. cit.*, p.117.

[27] Johnston, *op. cit.*, p. 32.

[28] Hetherington, *op. cit.*, p. 119.

[29] Johnston, *op. cit.*, p. 32.

Discipline was approved in 1561 by a meeting of nobles and burgesses, but it never received legal sanction from the civil magistrate.[30]   However, it was regarded as an accepted standard of the Church.

The Reformation spread rapidly throughout Scotland, and though in 1560 there were but twelve ministers in the kingdom, in 1567 there were 252 ministers, as well as 467 readers and 154 exhorters.[31] The seven years from 1560 to 1567 had been a period of struggle for the Protestant party in the State and the Reformed Church, against a government determined to undermine the Church by craft. During this period the Church had a double task-to provide for the evangelization and spiritual nurture of the nation, and to defend itself against the plots and attacks of Rome. By 1567 the Church of Scotland had the situation well in hand, and its General Assembly possessed great prestige in the kingdom.

5.   The Relation between Church and State, 1560-1567.

On December 25th, 1567, the General Assembly met and appointed commissioners to meet with six members of Parliament for the determination of Church matters and the jurisdiction of the Church.[32] For seven years the Church of Scotland had been independent of the State,[33] and now it became "established" in a certain sense. The Church of Scotland did not derive its existence from any act of Parliament, but was recognized by the Parliament as possessing and exercising inherent and preexistent powers and jurisdiction. The authority of the Church was derived,

---

[30] *Ibid.*, p. 35.

[31] Hetherington, *op. cit.*, p. 119.

[32] *Ibid.*, p. 118.

[33] Johnston, *op. cit.*, p. 34.

not from Parliament or the civil magistrate, but from Christ, the Head and King of the Church. The recognition of the Church by the State had the effect of ratifying and confirming the authority of the Church, and of protecting the Church from the assaults of its enemies.[34] This might be compared to the diplomatic recognition which one nation extends to another; such recognition does not create or originate the authority of the state that is recognized; it merely takes cognizance of a fact and gives formal and public recognition to that fact. Unlike the Church of England, the Church of Scotland was not a creature of the State, but a spiritual authority co-ordinate with the State and sovereign in its own sphere. During the first seven years of its existence, the Church of Scotland exercised supreme administrative and judicial powers, erected Synods, gave existence to presbyteries and sessions, and sanctioned the office of ruling elder, all by virtue of its own inherent authority derived not from the civil magistrate but from Christ alone.[35]

In 1567 Parliament ordained that the Church had the sole power of examination and admission of ministers, although the right of presentation of lay patronages was reserved to the ancient patrons.[36] Commissioners were appointed by Parliament to determine more exactly what causes came within the sphere of the judgment of the Assemblies of the Church.[37] The Church, while recognized by the State, and established as the only legally recognized Church in Scotland, exhibited a spirit of freedom and self-determination quite different from the attitude of the Protestant Churches in those countries of Europe where Erastian establishments prevailed.

[34] Hetherington, *op. cit.*, p. 118.

[35] *Ibid.*, p. 119.

[36] *Ibid.*, p. 117.

[37] *Ibid.*

CHAPTER II

STRUGGLES BETWEEN PRESBYTERY AND PRELACY, 1567- 1637

1.   Introduction of Tulchan Bishops, 1572.

The great scarcity of ministers at the beginning of the Reformation in Scotland, and the then condition of the Church throughout Scotland, influenced the General Assembly, under the leadership of John Knox, to provide for the offices of "readers" and "superintendents". Neither was intended to be more than a temporary expedient to meet the existing extraordinary situation. The emergency, created by the abolition of the Church of Rome in Scotland, had to be met. The "superintendents" were not really prelates at all in the ordinary sense of that term but extraordinary officers responsible to the judicatories of the Church.

In 1572, the Convention of Leith, a private assembly, unwittingly laid the foundations of prelacy in Scotland. The Convention proposed a compromise by which certain Episcopal titles would be permitted under the control of the General Assembly. The real motive for this proposal was the desire of the nobility to obtain for themselves the revenues of the Episcopal offices. The proposed bishops were to be members of Presbyteries, equal and not superior to their brethren in voting power, but holding the title of "Bishop".[1] It was the custom at that time in the Highlands of Scotland to

---

[1] Johnston, John C., *Treasury of the Scottish Covenant*, p. 43.

stuff a calf's skin with straw, and to place this before a cow while being milked, to induce the cow to give more milk. The stuffed calf was called a "tulchan", whence the new order of bishops created in 1572 were called "tulchan bishops".

When the proposal was under consideration in 1572, Patrick Adamson opposed the plan.[2] James Melville said that Adamson opposed the proposal because he was disappointed at not getting one of the bishoprics himself.[3] Adamson, who later reversed his position, said that there were "three sorts of bishops; my Lord Bishop, my Lord's Bishop, and the Lord's Bishop. My Lord Bishop was in the papistrie; my Lord's Bishop is now, when my Lord gets the benefice, and the bishop serves for nothing but to make his title sure; and the Lord's Bishop is the true minister of the gospel".[4]

Knox opposed the tulchan bishops, and refused to assist at the installation of one of them. He even pronounced an anathema against the new bishop and against the giver of the office, and when the General Assembly met Knox openly opposed the whole plan of tulchan episcopacy.[5] Nevertheless he was unsuccessful and the tulchan bishops remained.

2.   Andrew Melville, leader against Prelacy.

It has been held by some that it was not Knox, but Andrew Melville, who first taught in Scotland the doctrine of the divine right of Presbytery.[6] While this may be unfair to Knox, at any rate there can be no doubt that Andrew Melville

---

[2] Hetherington. W. M., *History of the Church of Scotland*, p. 130.

[3] *Ibid.*; Melville's Diary, p. 25.

[4] Hetherington, *op. cit.*, p. 130; Calderwood, p. 55.

[5] Hetherington, *op. cit.*, p. 130.

[6] Stanley, Arthur Penrhyn, *Lectures on the History of the Church of Scotland, Delivered in Edinburgh in 1872*, p. 48.

was the great champion of the divine right of Presbytery and the great opponent of Prelacy. In 1575 Melville, lately returned to Scotland from Geneva, spoke before the General Assembly, and argued on the basis of the Greek New Testament that the title of "Bishop" belonged to every minister of the gospel. Melville was sustained by the Assembly in this proposition.[7]

Andrew Melville was not only a man of great courage, but a man of great learning. His boldness and uncompromising spirit caused him to be summoned, in 1584, to appear before the Privy Council to answer for what were alleged to be treasonable speeches and prayers. Melville appeared before the council, protested against their summons, and boldly claimed the right of freedom of speech and the autonomy of the Church in spiritual matters.[8]

Melville's most famous saying is his admonition to King James VI in 1596. Melville was one of a group of ministers sent to confer with the monarch. The king had a mind of his own about the government of the Church and was not inclined to make any concessions. Melville took the king by the sleeve and told him to listen to what the ministers had to say, and addressed him thus: "Sir, there are two kings and two kingdoms in Scotland: there is King James the head of this commonwealth, and there is Christ Jesus, the King of the Church, whose subject James the Sixth is, and of whose kingdom he is not a king, nor a lord, nor a head, but a member. We will yield to you your place, and give you all due obedience; but again I say you are not the head of the Church; you cannot give us that eternal life, which we seek for even in this world, and you cannot deprive us of it. Permit us then freely to meet in the name of Christ, and to

[7] Johnston, *op. cit.*, p. 44.

[8] *Ibid.*, p. 53.

attend to the interests of that Church of which you are a chief member".[9] Another account of the same conversation contains the following straightforward statement: " Sir, when ye was in your swaddling-clothes, Christ reigned freely in this land, his ministers and servants did then freely in his name what they ought to do; and now, when ye are come to the kingdom, will ye take it upon you to make encroachments?"[10]

3.   Anti-Prelatic Actions of the General Assembly.

Andrew Melville was Moderator of the General Assembly of 1578. That Assembly, under Melville's leadership, adopted the Second Book of Discipline. It was never ratified by the civil magistrate, but was regarded as a lawful ecclesiastical standard of the Church of Scotland.[11] This standard sets forth pure Presbyterianism as the Scriptural form of Church government. The Second Book of Discipline was sworn to in the National Covenant in 1581. It was revised by the General Assembly of 1638, and although the book as a whole was never ratified by the civil power, its most important provisions were incorporated in civil legislation in 1592 and again after the Revolution in 1690.[12]

In 1580 the General Assembly met at Dundee. This Assembly condemned the office of bishop as without warrant in Scripture.[13] In 1582 the General Assembly passed an act declaring that no man can be admitted to ecclesiastical office

---

[9] *Ibid.*, p. 265.

[10] Walker, Patrick, *Six Saints of the Covenant*, I, p. 303. Cf. James Melvill's Diary, Wodrow Society, pp. 370-371.

[11] Johnston, *op. cit.*, p. 45.

[12] *Ibid.*, p. 47.

[13] *Ibid.*

by any civil magistrate or patron.[14]   In the same year the
General Assembly protested against the attempted
enforcement of Episcopacy by the State.[15]

In 1584 matters came to a crisis with the enactment of
the "Black Act" on May 22. Parliament sat behind closed
doors. All the anti-prelatic acts of the General Assembly were
declared to be treason. Parliament confirmed the king's
"royal power over all states and subjects within this realm".[16]
It was declared unlawful for the General Assembly to meet
without the royal consent. The ministers must acknowledge
the bishops as their superior officers. The nobility and gentry
yielded to these measures, but the ministers opposed them.[17]

During the next eight years, from 1584 to 1592,
Church government in Scotland was confused. A few
ministers left the country rather than submit to the new
legislation. The greater part submitted but felt wronged.
Prelacy and Presbytery were mixed together, the one existing
by authority of the King and Parliament, and the other by
authority of the General Assembly,[18]   that is, the authority of
Scripture as recognized by the General Assembly.

4.   The Great Charter of Presbytery, 1592.

The General Assembly met May 22nd, 1592, at
Edinburgh, and elected Robert Bruce as Moderator. King
James had returned from a visit to Norway, and was pleased
to note that the Church had promoted the peace of the country
during his absence, so he assumed a less unfavorable attitude

---

[14] *Ibid.*, p. 51.

[15] *Ibid.*, p. 52.

[16] *Ibid.*, pp. 53-54.

[17] *Ibid.*

[18] *Ibid.*, p. 54.

toward the Church than formerly. The Assembly thought it a good opportunity to press its matters, and accordingly drew up a list of requests and presented it to the King.[19] The Parliament met soon after, in June, and took up the requests. The result was the passing of an "Act for Abolishing of the Actis Contrair the Trew Religion".[20] This act did not grant all that the Church desired, but it was a great improvement over the existing state of affairs and far more satisfactory than any previous civil legislation.[21] The Act ratified and approved of General Assemblies, Synods, and Presbyteries, and the principal features of the Second Book of Discipline. It declared the "Black Acts" of 1584 to be "expired, null, and of none avail".[22] This Act of Parliament has been known as "The Great Charter of Presbytery". The law appointed General Assemblies to be held annually, or oftener if necessary; the time and place of the next meeting to be appointed by the King or his commissioner, or if neither should be present, by the assembly itself.[23] Lay patronage was retained, but ministers could be ordained or installed only by Presbyteries, which were to judge of the qualifications of candidates presented by patrons. In case a Presbytery should refuse to install a qualified candidate, presented by a patron, the patron could retain the fruits of the benefice himself.[24] It is interesting to note that the Act of 1592 abolished the observance of Christmas and Easter, which had been a grievance to the Church of Scotland: "Thairfor his Hienes and Estaittis foirsaidis has abrogat, cassit, and annullis, and be the tenor heirof, abrogatis, cassis and annullis.... Item. that pairt of the thirty-one Act maid be

---

[19] Hetherington, *op. cit.*, p. 163.

[20] Johnston, *op. cit.*, p. 54.

[21] Hetherington, *op. cit.*, p. 163.

[22] Johnston, *op. cit.*, p. 54.

[23] Hetherington, *op. cit.*, pp. 163-164.

[24] *Ibid.*

the Queene Regent, in the Parliament hadden at Edinburgh, the first day of Februar one thousand, five hundredth, fifty-ane zeirs, Geving speciall licence for haldin of Pashe and zule".[25]

Like the legislation of 1567, that of 1592 did not confer new powers on the Church of Scotland, but gave due legal recognition to the intrinsic powers of the Church. The Church had already (1578), in the Second Book of Discipline, asserted and claimed these powers as belonging to her by divine right and Scriptural warrant, and the law enacted by Parliament in 1592 served to recognize these powers and to protect the Church in the exercise of them.[26]

5.   Introduction of "Perpetual Moderators", 1607.

Not many years passed after 1592 before King James again attempted to force Prelacy on the Church of Scotland. In 1598 the General Assembly met at Dundee, and in some way the King persuaded the Assembly to agree to the appointment of commissioners to consult with the King. These commissioners were not to have the title of "Bishop" but they were to sit and vote in Parliament as the Catholic Bishops had done before the Reformation.[27] In 1599 the General Assembly agreed that the King should nominate the number and members of the commission, which those zealous for Presbytery called the "Woeful Commission".[28] In the end even the Episcopal title was given to these commissioners, in order to add dignity to power.[29]

---

[25] Johnston, *op. cit.*, p. 56.

[26] Hetherington, *op. cit.*, pp. 164-165.

[27] Johnston, *op. cit.*, p. 59.

[28] *Ibid.*

[29] *Ibid.*

The General Assembly of 1605 had been appointed by King James to meet in Aberdeen in July. During June the King sent out a circular notice postponing the meeting indefinitely. However nineteen ministers met at Aberdeen on July 2nd and constituted the Assembly, whereupon a messenger-at-arms appeared, who ordered the ministers to disperse upon pain of rebellion against the King. The Assembly agreed to dissolve on condition the King's representative would fix a date for the next meeting, but this was refused. Then the ministers appointed the next meeting to be held at the same place, on the last Tuesday of September of the same year.[30] This act on the part of the ministers was held to be rebellion, and for it sixteen ministers were imprisoned, and six convicted of treason and ordered banished. Although Andrew Melville had not been present at the meeting, he afterwards declared his approval of it, and for expression of opinion or belief he was confined to the Tower for three years, and finally released to allow him to become Professor of Divinity at Sedan in France.[31]

On July 1, 1606, forty-two ministers presented protestation to the Estates convened in Parliament, against the attempted intrusion of Prelacy on the Church of Scotland. Andrew Melville's name was at the head of the list.[32] This protestation put the ministers on record as opposing the King's policy, but had no other effect.

In 1607 "Perpetual moderators" were introduced. The King recommended that each Presbytery have a perpetual Moderator. The Bishops were made Moderators of such Presbyteries as usually met at Episcopal seats.[33] This

---

[30] *Ibid.*, p. 60.

[31] *Ibid.*, p. 61.

[32] *Ibid.*

[33] *Ibid.*, p. 65.

introduction of "Perpetual Moderators" was one of the final steps in King James' plan to foist complete diocesan Episcopacy on the Church of Scotland.

6.   Introduction of Complete Episcopacy, 1612.

In 1609 two Courts of High Commission were erected, one in Glasgow and the other in St. Andrews. The purpose of these courts was to enable the Bishops to enforce the powers which had been placed in their hands. Later the two courts were combined into a single tribunal with both civil and ecclesiastical powers. This court was not authorized by any act of Parliament, but only by the royal prerogative. No appeal could be taken from its decisions.[34] This move of King James was a piece of high-handed tyranny over the liberties, estates and, even the consciences of his subjects.

When the General Assembly met in Glasgow on the 8th of June, 1610, it proved to be a packed court. King James had sent letters to the several Presbyteries directing them whom to send as commissioners to the Assembly. When the Assembly met, bribery was freely used to influence the members in the King's favor. The Earl of Dunbar came from London with a large quantity of gold coins called "angels", from which circumstance the Assembly of 1610 was called the "Angelical Assembly".[35] These coins were distributed to the commissioners, ostensibly to defray their travelling expenses, as some had come from long distances. But Row records that "some neare Glasgow, who voted the King's way, got the wages of Balaam; while some gracious minister in the North, who voted negatively, got no gold at

---

[34] *Ibid.*

[35] *Ibid.*

all".[36]   In the end the King's prelatical proposals were carried, with but five negative votes. It was declared that the right of calling and dissolving Assemblies belonged to the royal prerogative; that Bishops were moderators of diocesan synods; that all presentations to benefices must be directed to the Bishops; that the Bishops possessed the powers of excommunication, absolution, and visiting the Churches in their dioceses.[37]

The Parliament in 1612 ratified the acts of the General Assembly of 1610, and in the process of ratification changed the acts to make them even more favorable to the Bishops, especially Spottiswoode, who claimed that the Act of Parliament of 1612 repealed the "Great Charter of Presbytery" of 1592.[38] The Parliament also declared that the King was the only lawful supreme ruler in Scotland, in all matters, both ecclesiastical and temporal. This Act of Parliament gave full legal sanction to diocesan Episcopacy in Scotland.[39]

The men who held the title of "Bishop" in Scotland in 1612 had not been properly consecrated and therefore did not have what was regarded as the true apostolical succession. Spottiswoode, Lamb and Hamilton were accordingly sent to London and there consecrated by the English Bishops. After they returned to Scotland, they in turn consecrated others, so as to give legitimacy to the Scottish Episcopate. This consecration of the Scottish Bishop took place without any warrant of either Parliament or the general Assembly.[40]

---

[36] *Ibid.*, p. 66.

[37] Hetherington, *op. cit.*, p. 218.

[38] *Ibid.*, p. 219; Spottiswoode, p.518.

[39] Johnston, *op. cit.*, pp. 66-67.

[40] *Ibid.*

In 1617, fifty-six ministers, who happened to be in Edinburgh on the occasion of King James' visit to Scotland at that time, submitted a formal protest against the King's publicly proclaimed intention to abolish the General Assembly of the Church of Scotland.[41] The independent spirit of the ministers of Scotland, though suffering from grievous wrongs, was still strong and eager to continue the conflict for the freedom and authority of the Church.

7.   The Five Articles of Perth, 1618.

The General Assembly of 1618 met at Perth on August 25th, the time and place having been appointed by the King. This was a packed court and a very tame, subservient one. The Prelates were in full control from the start. The Prelates, with the nobility and gentry, took all the seats that had been provided, and left the ministers to stand in the rear. No Moderator was elected as Spottiswoode claimed that as the Assembly was held in his diocese, it was his right to preside without an election.[42] When the famous "Five Articles of Perth" were about to be voted on, Spottiswoode even announced that the vote would be taken down and the names of all those voting in the negative would be sent to the King.[43] Although in the vote that followed the Articles were carried by a majority of about two to one, still forty-five ministers voted against them.[44]

The Articles thus adopted by the General Assembly provided for the following practices in the Church: Communion to be received in a kneeling posture; Private communion in cases of sickness; Private baptism in cases of

---

[41] *Ibid.*, p. 67.

[42] Hetherington, *op. cit.*, pp. 220-221.

[43] *Ibid.*

[44] *Ibid.*

necessity; catechising of young persons, and their being blessed by Bishops; and the observance of Christmas, Good Friday, Easter, Ascension and Pentecost, which were affirmed to be not merely Roman Catholic holy days but holy days of "the whole Kirk of the World".[45]

The Articles were ratified by the Parliament in 1621, and thereupon enforced by the Court of High Commission by civil penalties.[46] After Parliament had ratified the Articles, James wrote to the Prelates, telling them that now the sword was in their hands, and they should not let it rust.[47] It was ordained that ministers read the Articles from their pulpits, but not many complied with this order.[48] There was great indignation throughout Scotland on account of the Articles of Perth, which had been made not only the law of the Church but the law of the land.

8. The Controversy about the Book of Canons, 1636.

King James VI died in 1625 and was succeeded by Charles I, who continued James' policy of coercing the Church and nation of Scotland. Charles was not content with enforcing the Articles of Perth; he wished to introduce further changes into the public services of the Church. In 1633 the anti-prelatic ministers of Scotland addressed a petition to Charles, craving redress of grievances, but Charles saw nothing to redress and took no action.[49]

---

[45] Johnston, *op. cit.*, pp. 67-68.

[46] Hetherington, *op. cit.*, p.221.

[47] Johnston, *op. cit.*, pp. 67-68.

[48] *Ibid.*

[49] *Ibid.*, p. 73.

In September 1634 the Scottish Prelates decided to prepare a Book of Canons and also a liturgy for Scotland, and to send these to England, there to be revised by Laud and his colleagues. The Scottish Bishops did what they could on the Book of Canons, and then sent it to Archbishop Laud in England, who made some changes, after which the book was confirmed under the Great Seal, May 23, 1635. It was then sent to Scotland to be printed and circulated by the Bishops in their dioceses.[50] The book appeared in 1636, bearing the title "Canons and Constitutions Ecclesiastical for the Government of the Church of Scotland. Ratified and approved by his Majesty's royal Warrant", etc.[51] The design of this book was to introduce into Scotland the high, semi-Catholic Episcopacy of Laud. The first canon decreed excommunication against all who should deny the King's supremacy in ecclesiastical cases. The second canon decreed excommunication against all who should say that the form of worship in the (Scottish) Book of Common Prayer (not yet published) was superstitious or contrary to Scripture. Excommunication was also decreed again all who should say that Prelacy was unscriptural. Any minister who should fail to adhere to the proposed Liturgy was to be deposed. The General Assembly could not meet except at the call of the King. Ecclesiastical business could be discussed in no meetings except ecclesiastical courts presided over by Bishops. Ministers were forbidden to hold any private meetings for expounding Scriptures. Even extemporaneous prayer was put on the prohibited list.[52] There were also rules of a ceremonial nature. Baptismal fonts were to be placed near the Church doors. The consecrated elements must be carefully handled.[53] Ministers were asked to subscribe the

---

[50] Hetherington, *op. cit.*, p. 254.

[51] Johnston, *op. cit.*, p. 73.

[52] Hetherington, *op. cit.*, p. 73.

[53] Johnston, *op. cit.*, p. 73.

Book of Canons, and by doing so they pledged themselves to accept the prayer book which was to follow.[54] Burton says of the Book of Canons: "A complete code of laws for the government of a Church, issued by a sovereign without official consultation with the responsible representatives of that Church, is unexampled in European history".[55]

The people of Scotland were extremely indignant about the Book of Canons. The Prelates tried to defend it, but the advocates of Presbytery attacked it outspokenly. Although the common people held the book to be popish, no riots took place. The book was only partially enforced, and the real test of strength between the two parties did not take place until the following year when the Liturgy appeared.

9.   The Controversy about the Liturgy, 1637.

The Book of Canons was soon followed by the Liturgy. Even before the latter appeared, the Privy Council in December, 1636, ordered every parish in Scotland to have at least two copies.[56] The book was published at Edinburgh, 1637, under the title: "The Book of Common Prayer and Administration of the Sacraments and other Parts of divine Service for the use of the Church of Scotland".[57] The book had been prepared by two of the Scottish Bishops and then submitted to Laud, who made many changes. It was printed in a fine artistic style. "The book never made a martyr. No Episcopalian ever stood prepared to die for it. and it never survived the tumult of 1637".[58]

---

[54] *Ibid.*

[55] *Ibid.*; Burton, VI, p. 439.

[56] Johnston, *op. cit.*, p. 73.

[57] *Ibid.*, p. 74.

[58] *Ibid.*

Some of the features of the book most objectionable to Presbyterian consciences were the following: in the communion service, the table is called the "alter"; in consecrating the sacred elements, the minister was to stand with his back to the congregation; the cloth used to cover the elements was called a "corporal", that is, a burial cloth; some portions from the Apocrypha were included in the lessons; and the calendar contained a number of days commemorative of mediaeval saints.[59] These and similar features led the people of Scotland to conclude that the Liturgy was "popish", although modern Episcopal writers have maintained that it was more Protestant and less Roman than the English Prayerbook.[60] But with the people of Scotland it was not a question of less popery or more; they did not want any at all. It is probably quite true that many features of the book would have been regarded as quite harmless by some of the Reformed Churches on the Continent, but the fact is that the Church of Scotland had taken higher ground, and made a cleaner sweep of corruptions in worship, than any of these, and what had been fairly won they did not wish to surrender. Several of the Continental Reformed Churches never repudiated the observance of Christmas and Easter, but these had been made unlawful in the Church of Scotland in 1592 and the people resented the fact that they had been restored by the Articles of Perth in 1618. The Articles of Perth were bad enough, but when the Book of Canons was added in 1636 and the Liturgy in 1637, the country's patience neared the breaking point.

On June 13th, 1637, the Privy Council ordered all ministers to furnish themselves with two copies of the Service Book, within fifteen days, on pain of rebellion.[61]

---

[59] *Ibid.*

[60] Stanley, *op. cit.*, p. 49.

[61] Johnston, *op. cit.*, p. 76.

This action did not however order the use, but merely the purchase, of the books. The crisis came on July 23rd, 1637, in St. Giles Cathedral, Edinburgh, when Dean Hannay attempted to read the new Liturgy for the first time in Edinburgh. The people were tense with suppressed excitement. Suddenly a woman in the congregation took matters in her own hands and hurled the stool on which she was sitting at the Dean's head with the exclamation: "Villain, dost thou say mass at my lug?"[62] This was the signal for a general, though certainly unpremeditated, tumult. Bibles and stools were hurled at the Dean from all sides and he was glad to make his escape from the building. Later order was restored by the authorities, the doors closed, and the service resumed without further interruption.

On August 25th the Privy Council decided definitely that it was compulsory to purchase the Service Book but not compulsory to use it.[63] The same day the Privy Council addressed a letter to the King stating that the situation in Scotland was such that they would go no further without his express command.[64] The King's reply was dated September 10th. The King had been influenced by Laud, and reproved the Privy Council for suspending the compulsory use of the Service Book, and ordered its immediate resumption.[65] This message was received in Scotland with great indignation; multitudes flocked to Edinburgh. A company consisting of a hundred ministers and a large number of noblemen and gentry, marched in a body to the Privy Council on September 20th to petition against the Service Book.[66] The Council answered this petition on October 17th, by three

---

[62] Hetherington, *op. cit.*, p. 260.

[63] Johnston, *op. cit.*, p. 76.

[64] *Ibid.*

[65] *Ibid.*, pp. 76-77.

[66] *Ibid.*

proclamations in the King's name: (1) Strangers must leave the city, on pain of rebellion; (2) The Council and Supreme Court to be removed from Edinburgh; (3) A condemnation of a book entitled "Dispute against the English Popish Ceremonies", by George Gillespie.[67] By these proclamations the patience of the people was further tried. The following day, the "Noblemen, Gentrie, Ministers, Burgesses, and Commons" filed with the Council another protest against the Service Book and the Book of Canons.[68] The destiny of the Church of Scotland hung in the balances. Presbyterian government was gone; Presbyterian worship was about to be destroyed. If the constitution and worship of the Church of Scotland as by law established in 1592 was to be saved from total destruction, it was necessary that decisive action be taken by the friends of Presbyterian government and Scriptural worship. This action was taken and the Church was saved.

---

[67] *Ibid.*, p. 77.

[68] *Ibid.*

CHAPTER III

THE PERIOD OF THE SECOND REFORMATION, 1637—1651

1. The "Four Tables", 1637.

The Privy Council was called to meet at Edinburgh on November 15th, 1637. Before that day came, large numbers of loyal Presbyterians gathered in the city, which caused the Council to be alarmed. When the Council met, it asked the nobles to persuade the people to return to their homes. To this the nobles agreed, with the provision that a number should remain in the capital to transact business as the representatives of the rest. It was arranged that as many nobles as pleased, together with two gentlemen from each county, one minister from each Presbytery and one burgess from each burgh, should be   organized as a commission to represent the whole body of Presbyterians of Scotland. This body was to meet only on special occasions, while a part of them were to remain permanently in the capital to keep a watchful eye on developments. Those chosen to remain in the city were sixteen persons, consisting of four representatives each of the nobility, gentry, ministers and burgesses. As these four groups or committees sat in four different rooms of the Parliament building in Edinburgh, they came to be called "The Four Tables".[1] It was further arranged that one member from each of the Four Tables should constitute a supreme Table of four persons. In this way a very efficient organization was speedily set up. When this was completed, the multitudes of Presbyterians who were not residents of Edinburgh returned to their homes.[2]

The Four Tables soon proved themselves capable of activity. They complained to the Privy Council about the

---

[1] Hetherington, W. M., *History of the Church of Scotland*, p. 269.

[2] *Ibid.*, p. 270.

Prelates, the Book of Canons and the Service Book. The Privy Council tried to persuade them to drop the complaint against the Prelates, and press only those against the Canons and Liturgy, but this the Tables refused to do.[3] When the Council tried to avoid receiving the petition of the Tables at all, the latter practically compelled the Council to receive their representative's and hear their complaints.

It was the conviction of Presbyterian Scotland that if the King only had accurate knowledge of the situation in Scotland he would afford them some relief. The Prelates, however, and in particular Archbishop Laud, saw that the King was kept prejudiced in favor of their measures and against the Presbyterians. Laud advised the King to use force, and declared that if this were done, the Presbyterians would soon yield. The King acted on Laud's advice, and on February 20th, 1638, the King's Proclamation was posted at Stirling, declaring "that the bishops were unjustly accused as being the authors of the Service Book and Canons, seeing whatever was done by them in that matter was by his Majesty's authority and orders".[5] In addition to this, the King's Proclamation approved of the Canons and Service Book, and forbade all meetings and subscriptions against them, on pain of rebellion, and ordained that no petitioner appear in any town where the Privy Council was sitting, on pain of treason.[6]

2.   The National Covenant of Scotland, 1638.

The Proclamation at Stirling proved, for the first time, that not merely the Prelates, but the King himself, was

---

[3] *Ibid.*, p. 271.

[4] *Ibid.*, pp. 271ff.

[5] *Ibid.*

[6] *Ibid.*

determined to subvert the constitution and worship of the Church of Scotland. If absolutism in both Church and State was to be averted, immediate, strong and united action would be necessary. Among the ministers, Henderson, Dickson and others believed that the nation and the Church were guilty of serious defections, and that no real relief could be expected without repentance, confession of sin and renewed obedience to God and his law.[7] They announced a public fast, and invited ministers to deliver addresses on such subjects as the defections of the Church and nation of Scotland, confession of sins, and renewal of the Covenant of 1580-1581. At a meeting held on February 26th, 1638, it was determined to renew the Covenant, and that the document should be drawn up by Alexander Henderson and Johnston of Wariston, and revised by Rothes, Loudon and Balmerino.[8] Great care was taken in the preparation of the form of the Covenant, objections were attended to, and the whole revised, to avoid injury to anyone's conscience. Finally all objectors were satisfied.[9]

The completed Covenant consisted of three parts: (1) The Covenant of 1580-1581, *verbatim* ; (2) A legal section, consisting in an enumeration of the Acts of Parliament condemning popery and recognizing and ratifying the acts of the General Assembly. This part of the Covenant was compiled by Johnston; (3) The practical section, or special application of the whole to the existing circumstances. This part was drawn up by Henderson.[10]

The Covenant was publicly sworn on February 28,

---

[7] *Ibid.*, p. 275.

[8] *Ibid.*, pp. 275ff.

[9] *Ibid.*

[10] *Ibid.*, p. 276.

1638. The first meeting was held at daybreak: at this time the entire Covenant was read to the assembled congregation, and all objections were heard and answered. It was announced that the Covenant would be sworn and signed at the afternoon meeting, to be held in Greyfriars Church. At the appointed time the Covenant, written on parchment and ready for signatures, was produced. The meeting was first opened with prayer by Henderson. The Earl of Loudon then explained and defended the nature of the meeting, after which Johnston read the Covenant to the people again. After this there was a season of silence, and then Rothes announced that if there were still those who had doubts or scruples, they should state them and they would be answered. Loudon and Dickson would be at the west door of the Church to answer doubts for those from the west and south parts of Scotland, and Henderson and Rothes at the east door to answer for those from the north and east. "Few came, proposed but few doubts, and these few were soon resolved".[11] There was another season of silence, and finally the aged Earl of Sutherland came forward and affixed the first signature. After this the nobles present in the Church signed in turn.[12] On a later occasion the Covenant was signed by the ministers, and still later it was signed by large numbers of people of all classes throughout Scotland.

By the National Covenant of 1638, Scotland renewed the national renunciation of Popery, pledged adherence to Presbyterianism, and showed King Charles I that he was not above the law, and that so long as he observed the law of the land, he could count on the loyalty of the Scottish people. It has sometimes been held that the National Covenant was illegal and treasonable; but even a casual examination of the Covenant is sufficient to show that it was, in one of its

---

[11] *Ibid.*, p. 277.

[12] *Ibid.*

aspects, an appeal from the tyrynny of the King to the law of the land. That the Covenant was an agreement to resist tyranny cannot be denied: but this could not be illegal or treason, because Scotland was by law constituted a limited and not an absolute monarchy.

3. Royal Opposition to Ecclesiastical Reform, 1638.

The Covenant was signed on February 28th, 1638, and the General Assembly met on the 21st of November following. The intervening months were a time of conflict between King Charles I and the Covenanting party in Scotland. The King appointed the Marquis of Hamilton as Lord High Commissioner to represent the King in dealing with the people of Scotland. On May 16th the King sent Hamilton his instructions, listed in twenty-eight items, and closing with these words: "If you cannot by the means prescribed by us bring back the refractory and seditious to due obedience, we do not only give you authority, but command all hostile acts whatsoever to be used against them...for the doing whereof we will not only save you harmless, but account it as acceptable service done us".[13] On June 11th the King wrote to Hamilton again and said, "I will rather die than yield to those impertinent and damnable demands (as you rightly call them), for it is all one as to yield to be no king in a very short time".[14] To this letter the following postscript was added: "As the affairs are now, I do not expect that you should declare the adherers to the Covenant traitors, until you have heard from me that my fleet hath set sail for Scotland, though your six weeks should be elapsed. In a word, gain time, by all the honest means you

---

[13] Johnston, John C., *Treasury of the Scottish Covenant*, p. 86.

[14] *Ibid.*, pp. 86-87.

can, without forsaking your grounds".[15] This was followed
two days later by another letter to Hamilton, in which the
King wrote: "One of the chief things you are to labor now, is
to get a considerable number of Sessioners and Advocates to
give their opinion that the Covenant is at least against law, if
not treasonable. Thus you have my approbation in several
shapes".[16]

A Royal Proclamation was issued under date of June
28th, and read on July 4th at Edinburgh. In this Proclamation
the King seemed to make some concessions to the
Covenanters: "We do hereby assure all men that we will
neither now nor hereafter press the practice of the Canons and
Service Book, but in such a fair and legal way as shall satisfy
all our loving subjects".[17]   The Covenanters suspected that
this was merely a device to gain time; they were prepared,
and read a Protestation immediately after the reading of the
King's Proclamation.[18]

On September 9th another Royal Proclamation was
made, which purported to grant all that the Covenanters
desired. A free General Assembly should be held, followed
by a free Parliament. The Book of Canons, Service Book,
Court of High Commission, and Articles of Perth were to be
abolished. The General Assembly was to be allowed to try
the Prelates. The King would be favorable to the
Covenanters, and those who had opposed the King would be
pardoned.[19] That this Proclamation was insincere is shown
by the fact that on October 20th the King wrote to Hamilton
that he did not think that Episcopal government was in great

---

[15] *Ibid.*

[16] *Ibid.*, p. 87.

[17] *Ibid.*

[18] *Ibid.*

[19] *Ibid.*

danger in Scotland,[20] and also by the fact that when the General Assembly met, the King's Commissioner refused to sanction the trial of the Prelates.[21]

On September 22nd the Covenanters replied to the King's Proclamation of the 9th, in a document entitled "The Protestation of the Noblemen, Barons, Gentlemen, Burrowes, Ministers, and Commons". They objected that the proposed General Assembly would not be really free to act, and listed fifteen reasons why the King's Proclamation could not satisfy them, followed by seven protests. The Protestation was read by Archibald Johnston at Edinburgh.[22] On October 20th the King wrote to Hamilton: "I see by yours of the 27th September, that the malignity of the Covenanters is greater than ever. I will say confidently that until at least the adherers to this last Protestation be declared traitors nothing will go as it ought in that kingdom. As for the danger that Episcopal government is in, I do not hold it so much as you do.[23] The King spoke one language in his Proclamations to the Covenanters, and quite another in his secret letters to his Commissioner in Scotland.

4.   The General Assembly of 1638.

The General Assembly met in Glasgow Cathedral on Wednesday, November 21st, 1638. It was composed of 140 ministers, 2 professors, and 98 ruling elders. Of the elders, 17 were noblemen, 9 were knights, and the rest proprietors of land and burgesses. The Assembly sat until December 20th and initiated a thorough reformation of the Church of Scotland. This was the first free General Assembly held for

---

[20] *Ibid.*, p. 88.

[21] *Ibid.*, p. 93.

[22] *Ibid.*, p. 88.

[23] *Ibid.*

thirty-six years: in 1606, 1608, 1610, 1616, 1617 and 1618 nominal Assemblies had been held, but they were not free Assemblies, but completely under the control of the State, and later declared null and void.[24]

The Assembly proceeded to the trial of the Prelates and summoned these to appear at its bar to be judged. The Prelates refused to appear, and declined the authority of the Assembly in a document which they sent it, entitled "The Declinator and Protestation of the Archbishops and Bishops of the Church of Scotland and Others their Adherents, Agaynst the pretended Generall Assemblie at Glasgow, 1638".[25] In this paper they declared that the meeting was "most unlawful and disorderly" and so they would not attend.[26] After the declinature of the Prelates, the Moderator, Alexander Henderson, asked the Assembly whether it found itself a court competent to sit in judgment on the Prelates. At this point the King's Commissioner forbade any further proceedings and ordered the immediate dissolution of the Assembly.[27] Hamilton in the King's name called on Henderson to dissolve the meeting with prayer, and when Henderson refused to do so, Hamilton himself declared the meeting dissolved and forbade all further sessions. This was the 29th of November.[28] The Assembly, however, refused to be dissolved, and prepared a "Protestation" against the King's Commissioner's Proclamation dissolving the Assembly.[29] The same day a Royal Proclamation was issued against the Assembly; it was called a "pretended Assembly", its members "pretended commissioners"; and they were

[24] *Ibid.*, pp. 88-92.
[25] *Ibid.*, pp. 92-93.
[26] *Ibid.*
[27] *Ibid.*
[28] *Ibid.*, p. 93.
[29] *Ibid.*, p. 94.

ordered to leave the city within twenty-four hours. The Assembly, however, was not to be intimidated, and continued to meet for three more weeks.

When the Assembly finally adjourned, it had carried through an extensive reform of the Church. Prelacy was declared unlawful, and Presbytery restored. The Bishops and Archbishops were excommunicated. The Articles of Perth were declared unlawful. The Assembly condemned the Book of Canons, Liturgy, Book of Ordination, and the Court of High Commission; and the Assemblies held from 1606 to 1618 were declared null and void because of royal interference with their freedom.[31] The Assembly had reasserted the freedom and authority of the Church, had renounced Erastian, Prelatic and sacramentarian corruptions, and had declared boldly against tyrannical abuse of power in both Church and State.

5.   Continued Royal Opposition to Reform.

The General Assembly met again in August, 1639, and issued an act enumerating six causes "of the Bygone Evils of this Kirk", as follows: (1) The forcing of the Liturgy on the Church; (2) The Articles of Perth; (3) Substitution of government by Prelates for General Assemblies; (4) The civil powers of the Prelates; (5) Corrupt Assemblies; and (6) The lack of free and rightly constituted Assemblies. This act was passed by the animous vote of the General Assembly, and the King's Commissioner promised to hand in to the clerk his written consent.

Meanwhile King Charles I was becoming alarmed

---

[30] *Ibid.*

[31] *Ibid.*, pp. 94-95.

about the situation in Scotland.   In 1639 he marched with his forces towards Scotland, and circulated a document called the "Short Declaration", in which he justified his resort to the use of armed force against Scotland, spoke of his "divine right", and said that the Covenant was a "conspiracy"; he said that the Covenant "could not be with God, being against us, the Lord's anointed over them".[33] Later in the year the "Large Declaration" appeared, a document still more violent than the "Short Declaration".[34] The Scotch prepared to defend their country and Church against the King, and raised an army for this purpose. The Covenanters under General Leslie encamped at Dunse Law, about six miles from the King's forces. It was on this occasion that the blue banner of the Covenanters was first flown; the banner displayed the national arms and also the words "FOR CHRIST'S CROWN AND COVENANT" in gilt letters.[35] When King Charles saw the determination of the Scotch, he decided to treat with them. A treaty was signed on June 18th, after which the forces on both sides were disbanded. By the treaty the King agreed, among other things, that a General Assembly and a Parliament should be held at Edinburgh in August, to determine the matters of the Church and the nation.

When the General Assembly met the following year (August, 1640) it enacted that persons who had subscribed the Covenant, and later spoke against it, should be dealt with by ecclesiastical censures. A minister was to be deposed, and later excommunicated; a layman, to be disciplined for perjury.[37] In 1641 the Scottish Parliament made the Covenant

---

[32] *Ibid.*, pp. 95-96.

[33] *Ibid.*, p. 96.

[34] *Ibid.*

[35] Hetherington, *op. cit.*, p. 317.

[36] *Ibid.*, p. 318.

[37] Johnston, *op. cit.*, p. 96.

a civil test: none could take his seat in Parliament until he took the Covenant. A number of noblemen were excluded from the Parliament chamber until they subscribed the Covenant.[38] The same Parliament ratified the action of the General Assembly abolishing Prelacy, approved the Covenant, and restored to the statute book the "Great Charter of Presbytery" of 1592.[39]

6. The Solemn League and Covenant, 1643.

The Long Parliament of England began in 1640. By 1642 England was involved in civil war between the King and the Parliament. In August, 1643, the Parliament of England proposed to the Estates of Scotland, and also to the General Assembly of the Church of Scotland, that Scotland enter into a reciprocal military union with the Parliamentary party in England. The Church of Scotland, however, preferred a religious bond to a military or civil union. The result was the drafting of the Solemn League and Covenant. The document was prepared by Alexander Henderson, and on the 17th of August, 1643, it was approved by the General Assembly of the Church of Scotland, after which it was sent to England, where, after slight changes,[40] it was publicly sworn and afterwards subscribed by the House of Commons and the Westminster Assembly in a joint meeting. After this the Solemn League and Covenant was returned to Scotland, where it was sworn and subscribed by the Commission of the General Assembly of the Church of Scotland, and the Committee of the Convention of Estates of the Parliament of Scotland. Later it was sworn and subscribed with great unanimity by all classes of people throughout Scotland,

---

[38] *Ibid.*

[39] *Ibid.*

[40] Cheetham,S., *A History of the Christian Church Since the Reformation*, p.34.

except those who favored Prelacy in the Church and
absolutism in the State.

The Solemn League and Covenant provided for the
preservation of the Reformed religion in Scotland, and the
reformation of religion in England and Ireland according to
the Word of God, and the example of the best Reformed
Churches. The Covenant also pledged the parties to the
extirpation of Popery and Prelacy. The precise nature of the
reformation to be attained was not stated, nor did the
document state which Churches were the "best Reformed
Churches". However it was generally understood that the
bodies holding the Presbyterian system of government were
intended, for the Church of Scotland was committed to the
position that Presbytery is the only system of Church
government set forth in the Word of God.

In 1644 the General Assembly enacted that all
ministers take notice of any persons disaffected to the
National Covenant or the Solemn League and Covenant who
should come within the bounds of their parishes, so that these
persons could be reported to the Presbyteries or other
ecclesiastical judicatories.[41] When King Charles I surrendered to the Scottish army in 1646 he declared his
disapprobation of the Solemn League and Covenant.[42]
Regulations were promulgated in Scotland by which large
numbers of people were required to sign or give their
approval of the document. In 1651 the Rev. James Guthrie
stated that one of the causes of the Lord's wrath against
Scotland was the ignorance and want of sincerity on the part
of many in taking the Covenants: "Many did take the national
covenant, in example of others, it being counted praiseworthy
and commendable, after such a defection as was then in the

---

[41] Johnston, *op. cit.*, p. 105.

[42] *Ibid.*, pp. 97-105.

land, to engage in such a duty, and to be reckoned amongst the repairers of the breach: many did take the solemn league and covenant, for fear; because the refusing to take it was attended both with ecclesiastical and civil censures, and therefore did they rather choose to hazard on the oath of God, than to run these hazards amongst men: which doth not yet condemn the enjoining the taking of these covenants upon a good and warrantable principle.... In taking of both covenants, though there were many whom a principle of the fear and love of God did move, yet there were not a few, whom after discoveries have made manifest, who were acted thereto by carnal wisdom and policy, for attaining their own base and corrupt ends, such as riches, places of preferment, and livelihood, and ease...".[43] Guthrie listed as one of the special sins of the ministers of Scotland "Superficial admitting of all to the covenants; and solemn acknowledgment without taking sufficient pains to instruct and inform them in the knowledge of the things contained therein".[44] This testimony of Guthrie that many took the Covenants as a mere formality, or at best with an implicit faith, is not difficult to believe when we realize that such subscription was required of students entering colleges, of all persons for the first time receiving the Lord's Supper, as well as of other special classes of persons.[45] The Scotch later urged Charles II to sign the Covenants when at least some of them were sure he was playing the hypocrite. The leaders of Scottish Presbyterianism had not yet learned that subscription of a religious covenant, to be honest, must be voluntary and not the result of external pressure of any kind. Guthrie justified the infliction of both ecclesiastical and civil censures on those who refused to take the Solemn League and

---

[43] *Testimony Bearing Exemplified* (Paisley, 1741; New York, 1843), pp. 122-124.

[44] *Ibid.*, p. 175.

[45] Johnston, *op. cit.*, p. 116.

Covenant, and yet he counted it a cause of the Lord's wrath
that so many took the Covenant insincerely or from wrong
motives.[46] It seems strange that neither he, nor, apparently,
anyone else at that time, could see that when refusal to take
the Covenant was attended with civil censures, it would
require extraordinary force of character and incorruptible
honesty to refuse to take the Covenant. It is difficult to avoid
the conclusion that the Parliament of Scotland and the General
Assembly unintentionally tempted many to accept the
Covenants in a dishonest, careless, or at least implicit way.
Of course Scotland professed to be a Reformed nation, and
certainly such nation has the right, by its own voluntary act,
to make a religious test essential to the holding of public
office under its constitution; but when, for example, none
could enter an institution of higher learning as a student
without accepting the Covenant, it must be concluded that the
zeal of the Covenanter leaders exceeded their wisdom, and
that they placed a strong temptation to dishonesty or implicit
belief in the pathway of many in the land.

7.   The Westminster Assembly, 1643-1649.

On June 1st, 1642, the Long Parliament of England
passed a bill to call an Assembly of Divines for consultation
with Parliament; this bill, and two others like it, failed to
obtain the consent of the King. Finally, in 1643, the
Parliament called such an assembly by a Parliamentary
ordinance, which did not require the King's consent. The
Assembly was called to meet on July 1st, 1643, for the
purpose of advising Parliament to the end of settling the
government of the Church of England according to Scripture
and clearing the doctrine of the Church of England from all
false calumnies and aspersions.

---

[46] *Testimony Bearing Exemplified*, p. 124.

After the Westminster Assembly had sat for some weeks Commissioners from the Church of Scotland were added to its membership. The Scottish Commissioners originally appointed consisted of four ministers (Rutherford, Douglas, Baillie and Gillespie) and three ruling elders (John, Lord Maitland, afterwards Duke of Lauderdale, Archibald Johnston of Wariston, and John, Earl of Cassilis). Later in the history of the Assembly, other Scottish Commissioners were added. Apart from the Scottish Commissioners, the Assembly ultimately had about 150 members. Of these, some thirty were members of Parliament, and the others were ministers representing the various parties of the Church of England, with the exception of the Romanizing party of Archbishop Laud.

Before the date set for the first meeting of the Assembly, it was forbidden to meet by a proclamation of King Charles I. A large number of the persons appointed met, however, in spite of the King's proclamation, and proceeded to transact business.

The Westminster Assembly itself really belongs to English rather than to Scottish Church history, yet the Church of Scotland cooperated in the enterprise at the time, and the work of the Assembly has had far greater permanent effects in Scotland than in England. The chief doctrinal standards of all branches of Scottish Presbyterianism down to the present day were formulated by the Westminster Assembly of Divines. The standards prepared by the Assembly include a "Form of Presbyterial Church-Government", a "Directory for the Public Worship of God", and the famous Confession of Faith and Larger and Shorter Catechisms. All of these were prepared "as parts of the Covenanted uniformity in religion betwixt the Churches of Christ in the Kingdoms of Scotland,

England and Ireland".[47]

The Westminster Assembly sat from 1643 to 1649, after which it became a committee for the examination of ministers, in which capacity it continued to meet until 1652, when it was finally dissolved after the dissolution of the Long Parliament by Cromwell. The Westminster Standards were all adopted by the General Assembly of the Church of Scotland, and the Confession, Catechisms and Directory for Worship were ratified by the Scottish Parliament. The Scots Confession of Faith, which had been the doctrinal standard of the Church of Scotland since 1560, was thus superseded by General Assembly's adoption of the Westminster Confession in 1647.

The constitution given to the Church of Scotland by the adoption of the Westminster Standards was eminently Reformed in its three aspects -doctrine, worship and organization. The modern notion that while doctrine should be Scriptural, worship and organization are matters of indifference to be arranged according to expediency or human preference, was entirely foreign to the Westminster Assembly and the Church of Scotland of the period of the Second Reformation. Great stress was placed on the importance of Scriptural forms of worship and organization. Probably the Church of Scotland has suffered more than any branch of the Christian Church through the ages on account of insistence upon a pure and Scriptural form of organization.

It is worthy of note that when the Confession of Faith was adopted by the General Assembly in 1647, two reservations were carefully laid down by the Assembly. The first of these was "that the not mentioning in this Confession the several sorts of ecclesiastical officers and assemblies,

---
[47] Title pages of various editions of the Confession of Faith, etc.

shall be no prejudice to the truth of Christ in these particulars, to be expressed fully in the Directory of Government".[48] The second was "that the Assembly understandeth some parts of the second article of the thirty-first chapter only of Kirks not settled, or constituted in point of government: And that although, in such kirks, a synod of Ministers, and other fit persons, may be called by the Magistrate's authority and nomination, without any other call, to consult and advise with about matters of religion; and although, likewise, the Ministers of Christ, without delegation from their churches, may, of themselves, and by virtue of their office, meet together synodically in such kirks not yet constituted, yet neither of these ought to be done in kirks constituted and settled".[49] These reservations show the emphasis placed by the Church of Scotland upon Scriptural organization, and the great care taken not to commit the Church to anything in the Confession that could be understood in an Erastian sense.

8.   The Engagement, 1648.

The most prominent royalist in Scotland was the Duke of Hamilton. Charles I was a prisoner of the English Parliament, but the Scotch still maintained their loyalty to the King and were willing to do what they could for him, short of breach of the Solemn League and Covenant. In December, 1647, a party of Scottish noblemen visited the King secretly in the Isle of Wight, and made with him a secret treaty, by which Hamilton and his party agreed to raise an army in Scotland to assist the King in his effort to regain the throne of England. The King promised to permit the Solemn League and Covenant to be sanctioned by Parliament, and to support Presbyterian government in his dominions for three years,

---

[48] Act of the General Assembly of the Church of Scotland, Edinburgh, August 27, 1647, Session 23.

[49] *Idem.*

and after that, such form of Church government as should be determined by an assembly of divines aided by twenty commissioners nominated by himself. The King also undertook to suppress schism and heresy.[50] This treaty with the King was called the Engagement, and Hamilton and the nobles who joined with him were called the "Engagers".

When the fact of the Engagement began to be publicly known in Scotland, early in 1648, many of the Covenanters were opposed to the plan. In March the terms of the treaty were revealed to the Parliament, and a violent controversy followed. The Commission of the General Assembly met and issued a statement that the Engagement was sinful, involved perjury by breach of covenant vows, and would draw the displeasure of God on the Church and nation of Scotland.[51] The royalists were in control in the Scottish Parliament, and so the protests of the stricter Covenanters were disregarded and the nation plunged into the course which ultimately brought ruin upon Scotland. The Parliament passed an act requiring all subjects to sign a bond supporting the Engagement. When the General Assembly met in July 1648 the declaration of the Assembly's Commission was approved, and the Act of Parliament requiring the bond to support the Engagement was condemned. The Assembly also warned all members of the Church of Scotland to beware of the unlawfulness and dangers of the Engagement, and passed an act of censure on all ministers who had favored the Engagement or who had neglected to warn against its sinfulness. A letter was also sent to the King, asserting the sinfulness of the Engagement, and that the concessions he had promised were not adequate, and requesting him to comply with the Covenant so that they could consistently

---

[50] Hetherington, *op. cit.*, p. 348; Johnston, *op. cit.*, pp. 117-118.

[51] Hetherington, *op. cit.*, p. 349.

support and defend him.[52]

The army raised for the Engagement was led into England to fight the King's battles, and defeated by Cromwell at Preston. Hamilton, the commanding officer, was hanged. The Engagement thus failed of its purpose and came to nothing. But it had the effect of driving a wedge of division into the hitherto unbroken ranks of the Covenanters.

9. The Act of Classes, 1649.

The failure of the Engagement caused a political change in Scotland. The strict Covenanters obtained control of the Parliament, which had been controlled by the Engagers. The Covenanters were able to convince Cromwell that they had been opposed to the Engagement, and so hostilities between Cromwell and Scotland were averted for the time being. On January 4th, 1649, the Parliament passed the Act of Classes, which declared the Engagers to be Malignants and ineligible for public office.[53] The Act enumerated four classes of persons ineligible for public office, and classified these according to the degree of their disqualification.[54] The Army was purged of all persons who had taken part in the Engagement or were suspected of being Malignants, that is, opposed to the Covenants.[55] The Act of Classes has sometimes been regarded as an intolerant and unreasonable measure, but it must be remembered that it was a time of great public danger, and that the purpose of the law was to preserve the safety of the nation by keeping out of public office men who were known to be opposed to the recognized principles and sacred obligations of the nation.

---

[52] *Ibid.*, pp. 349-350.

[53] Johnston, *op. cit.*, pp. 117-118.

[54] Hetherington, *op. cit.*, p. 352.

[55] Johnston, *op. cit.*, pp. 119-120.

Nor should it be forgotten that Scotland professed to be a Christian and a Reformed nation, and as such possessed an unquestionable right to determine what classes of men were unfit to be rulers in such a nation. The philosophy which underlay the Act of Classes was the philosophy of Christian civil government, and Christian civil government cannot continue to exist in a wicked world without the provision of religious tests for public office.

10.   Negotiations with Charles II, 1650,

King Charles I was executed by the English Parliament in 1649. No doubt the attempt of the Scotch to help him by the Engagement hastened his miserable end. Early in 1650 the Scottish Parliament sent commissioners to the Continent to confer with Charles II on the basis of the Covenants. Charles sailed for Scotland, and landed on June 16th, 1650, but not until after he had subscribed the Solemn League and Covenant. Accompanying Charles were several men whom the Act of Classes had excluded from positions of public responsibility.[56] In August Charles signed a declaration renouncing Popery and Prelacy and professing adherence to the Solemn League and Covenant.[57] There can be little doubt, in view of later events, that Charles was hypocritical and that he would sign or swear anything if he could thereby further his own ends. Even in 1650 some of the Covenanting leaders suspected Charles of insincerity, but the majority seemed ready to accept a mere technical acceptance of the Covenants on the part of Charles, without any real evidence of sincere and hearty acceptance of the covenant bonds to which the Scottish Church and nation were pledged by oath. This readiness to receive Charles II proved the undoing of Scotland, for it soon brought on an invasion by Cromwell, who could not tolerate a Stuart and an enemy of the Commonwealth on the throne of Scotland.

---

[56] Hetherington, *op. cit.*, p. 357.

[57] *Ibid.*, pp. 357-358.

CHAPTER IV

THE CHURCH OF SCOTLAND UNDER THE COMMONWEALTH, 1651-1660.

1.   Scotland Subjected to the Commonwealth, 1650-1652.

The Battle of Naseby, June 14th, 1645, marked the destruction of the power of Charles I. Cromwell's victorious army placed its leaders in the highest offices in England. The English Parliament was alarmed that the Scotch received Charles II, and prepared to invade Scotland. Cromwell consulted the Psalms and then decided to take command of the invading army, confident that the Lord would "enable this poor worm and weak servant to do his will".[1] He entered Scotland the 22nd of July, 1650, with sixteen thousand soldiers and a fleet along the coast.[2] As the invaders approached Edinburgh they were opposed by the Scotch under General Leslie. At the battle of Dunbar, September 3rd, Cromwell attained a notable victory over the Scotch. Four thousand prisoners were sent to England; many of these died of disease on the way, and by November only 1,400 of them remained alive.[3]   On September 7th Cromwell's army captured Edinburgh.

On January 1st, 1651, Charles II was crowned King of Scotland at Scone. Considering the later life and activities of Charles II, it may not be amiss to quote the coronation oath which he swore at this time: "I, Charles, King of Great Britain, France and Ireland, do assert and declare, by my

---

[1] Hewison, J. King, *The Covenanters*, II, p. 3.

[2] *Ibid.*

[3] *Ibid.*, p. 15.

solemn Oath, in the Presence of Almighty God, the Searcher
of Hearts, my Allowance and Approbation of the National
Covenant, and of the Solemn League and Covenant, above
written, and faithfully oblige myself to prosecute the Ends
thereof in my Station and Calling; and that I for Myself and
Successors shall consent and agree to all Acts of Parliament
enjoining National Covenant and Solemn League and
Covenant, and fully establishing Presbyterial Government,
the Directory for Worship, Confession of Faith, Catechisms,
in the Kingdom of Scotland, as they are approven by the
General Assemblies of this Kirk, and Parliaments of this
Kingdom; and that I shall give my royal assent to Acts or
Ordinances of Parliament passed, or to be passed, enjoining
the same in my other Dominions: and that I shall observe
these in my own Practice and Family, and shall never make
Opposition to any of these, or endeavour any change
thereof".[4] A man who could take such an oath, and later order
copies of the Covenants to be burned by the hangman, and
order those who adhered to the Covenants to be tried for
treason, certainly holds a high rank among the great perjurers
of history.

In March, 1651, the Scottish Parliament made Charles
II commander-in-chief of the army. Although a large part of
Scotland was in Cromwell's hands, Charles II and General
Leslie invaded England in July of that year. The great battle
took place at Worcester. The Scotch had about 16,000 men,
and the English Parliamentary army twice as many.[5] It was
September 3rd, 1651, precisely a year after the battle of
Dunbar. The Scotch were again completely defeated by the
soldiers of the Commonwealth. Thousands of the Scotch
troops were taken prisoners or killed. The King escaped, and
after wandering about England for some weeks, finally

---

[4] *Ibid.*, p. 27.

[5] *Ibid.*, pp. 32-33.

reached France on October 16th, 1651, a miserable figure in utter poverty and dependent on the pity of his friends.[6] By May, 1652, all of Scotland was reduced to submission to the army of the Commonwealth.

Not long after the battle of Worcester, the English Parliament asserted the proprietorship of the Commonwealth in Scotland. England and Scotland were to be governed by a council of twenty-one members, of whom Cromwell was one. In 1652 commissioners were sent to Scotland to institute this government. The people of Scotland were strongly opposed to the Commonwealth, but they were powerless to resist it. All judicatories not licensed by Parliament were prohibited, and all oaths and covenants were forbidden unless sanctioned by the government. On February 4th, 1652, the royal arms were publicly destroyed at Edinburgh and the authority of Charles II was pronounced abolished.[7]

On February 13th, 1652, the commissioners proposed to the Scotch the "Tender", an offer of incorporation of Scotland with England. According to the terms of the proposal, ministers both of the established Church and of dissenting sects were to have freedom to preach. Although some of the Scotch favored the Tender, most of the ministers were against it. The Rev. James Guthrie opposed it and in consequence had soldiers quartered in his house.[8] The Presbytery of Dunfermline even advised against a marriage between an English soldier and a Scotch girl, because of the sinfulness of the Commonwealth.[9] Very few of the Scottish ministers ever signified their approval of the Tender.

---

[6] *Ibid.*

[7] *Ibid.*, pp. 40-41.

[8] *Ibid.*

[9] *Ibid.*

2.   The Controversy between Resolutioners and Protestors, 1650-1653.

After Cromwell's capture of Edinburgh in 1650, King Charles II and the royalists in Scotland determined to seek a more united support by the different parties in the Church and nation. The outcome of this determination was a proposal known as the "Public Resolutions". The Estates of Parliament consulted the General Assembly, whether some way could not be found by which those persons who had been disqualified by the Act of Classes could be restored to positions in the State and in the army. The General Assembly held in July, 1651, passed the Resolutions, and declared that "In this case of so great and ardent necessity, we cannot be against the raising of all fencible persons in the land, and permitting them to fight against this enemy for defence of the kingdom; excepting such as are excommunicated, forfeited, profane, flagitious", etc.[10] The "ardent necessity" to which the Assembly referred was the defeat of the Scottish army by Cromwell at the Battle of Dunbar, and the subsequent capture of Edinburgh. From July, 1651, on, the Covenanters were divided into Resolutioners and Protestors. Those who favored the Public Resolutions were called Resolutioners, and those who opposed them were called Protestors, because they protested against the legality of the General Assembly which had ratified the Public Resolutions.

The leaders of the Protestors were James Guthrie, Patrick Gillespie, Johnston of Wariston and Samuel Rutherford. Even before the adoption of the Resolutions, in September, 1650, these men published "A Shorte Declaratione and Varninge",[11] in which they called the land to

---

[10] Johnston, John C., *Treasury of the Scottish Covenant*, p. 120.

[11] Hewison, *op. cit.*, II, p. 17.

national repentance and especially called upon the King to repent for his sins, and especially to consider whether he had not been guilty of hypocritical acceptance of the Covenants in order to obtain the crown.

In later times it has been common to represent the controversy between the Resolutioners and the Protestors as a quarrel over trifles, an utterly unnecessary division of the forces of Presbyterianism. History has shown, however, that the Protestors were right and the Resolutioners wrong. Many of the persons admitted to power under the Public Resolutions become persecutors of Presbyterianism after 1660. If the Protestors had been able to control affairs Scotland might have been spared twenty-eight years of terrible persecution under the bloody and perjured Stuarts.

The question involved in the controversy was whether it was proper, under the existing circumstances, to repeal the Act of Classes. The General Assembly approved of such repeal, but with certain restrictions concerning the excommunicated, profane, etc. When this approval had been granted by the General Assembly, the Parliament repealed the Act of Classes entirely, taking no notice of the exceptions reserved by the Assembly. This opened the way for a flood of ungodly men and open enemies of the covenanted Reformation to receive places of responsibility in the government and army.

It is clear that the Resolutioners and the Protestors differed from each other not only in the specific matter of the propriety of the repeal of the Act of Classes, but in their whole view of the principles and ethics of Christian civil government. The Protestors viewed the calamities of the nation as the consequences of national sin. In their view, the remedy lay in repentance, confession of sin and a new obedience to the divine law. That is to say, they looked at the situation from the spiritual viewpoint and they were sure that not carnal, but spiritual remedies must be used if real relief was to be had. Along with this they maintained the Christian ethical principle that it is never right to do evil that good may come, that the end cannot justify the means, and that circumstances can never justify sin; and they applied these principles not merely to individual and ecclesiastical life, but to the life of the nation as such. They would obey God, put their trust in God, and leave the issue with God.

The Resolutioners, on the other hand, looked upon the national calamities as the result of lack of unity in the nation. In their view, the remedy lay in healing the breaches caused by the Act of Classes, and rallying all the people of Scotland to the defence of the King and the kingdom, regardless of differences in religion or past conduct. They looked at the situation from the worldly viewpoint, and wished to apply mechanical rather than spiritual remedies. They appear to have felt that whatever might be the abstract right or wrong of the thing, the national emergency justified overlooking such considerations and taking all possible measures against the enemy.

It may be said, too, that most of the really earnest Christians of Scotland were numbered in the ranks of the Protestors. Hetherington says that "the writings of the Protestors are thoroughly pervaded by a spirit of fervent piety, and contain principles of the loftiest order, stated in language of great force and even dignity, of which we find but few similar instances in the productions of the Resolutioners".[12]

The controversy between the two parties continued

[12] Hetherington, W. M., *History of the Church of Scotland*, pp. 366-367.

for a long time. In 1652 the Protestors held a General Assembly, and after their adjournment the Resolutioners held an Assembly, at which representatives of the Protestors appeared and handed in a protest signed by sixty-three ministers and eighty laymen, which declared the Resolutioner General Assembly to be "unlawful, unfrie and unjust".[13] The Resolutioner Assembly threatened to censure the Protestors but the latter obtained the protection of the Commonwealth. In 1653 the two parties held general Assemblies at the same time in the same building, St. Giles Cathedral, Edinburgh, with a partition between them.[14]

3. Cromwell Suppresses the General Assembly, 1653.

While the Resolutioner and Protestor Assemblies were meeting in July, 1653, Lieutenant-Colonel Cotterel, an officer in Cromwell's army, appeared on the scene with a body of soldiers, entered the Church, and inquired by whose authority the Resolutioner Assembly was sitting. Was it by authority of Charles II or of Cromwell?[15] The Moderator, David Dickson, replied, "We sit here by the authority of Jesus Christ and by the law of this land, whereby we are authorized to keep General Assemblies from year to year, according to the several Acts of Parliament, and every Assembly meets by appointment of the former".[16] Cotterel then ordered the Resolutioner General Assembly to leave the Church, and after he had led them a mile outside of Edinburgh, he released the commissioners, ordering them to depart to their homes on pain of being held for breach of the

---

[13] Hewison, *op. cit.*, II, p. 43.

[14] *Ibid.*, p. 44.

[15] Hetherington, *op. cit.*, p. 364.

[16] Hewison, *op. cit.*, II, p. 45.

peace.[17]

The Protestor General Assembly, which was meeting at the same time and place, was allowed to continue its sessions undisturbed for the time being. Later their meeting, too, was suppressed, and the Protestors published a protest against Cromwell's unlawful suppression of the General Assembly.[18]   From 1653 the General Assembly was forbidden to meet without permission from Parliament.[19]

4.   The State of the Church of Scotland under the Commonwealth.

In 1655 Cromwell gave official support to the Protestors, in the form of a commission given to Patrick Gillespie and others authorizing them to settle the affairs of the Church of Scotland.[20] After this the Protestors had the direct support of English troops to enforce their decisions on the Church. Cromwell gave orders that in the admission of ministers, the decision should be made by the most religious part of the people, even though not the majority.[21]

Through the period of the Commonwealth, Scotland enjoyed complete civil peace. The General Assembly was not permitted to meet, but apart from this the life and activities of the Church continued as usual. It was a time of spiritual revival and strengthening. James Kirkton wrote "I verily believe there were more souls converted to Christ in that short period of time than in any season since the Reformation,

[17] Hetherington, *op. cit.*, p. 364.

[18] Hewison, *op. cit.*, II, p. 46.

[19] Cheetham, *A History of the Christian Church Since the Reformation*, p. 47; Burnet, G., *History of His own Time*, I, p. 107.

[20] Hetherington, *op. cit.*, p. 365.

[21] *Ibid.*

though of triple its duration".[22]

The Protestors, though supported by Cromwell in their control of the Church, never acknowledged the right of his authority or that of the Commonwealth. It is probable that Patrick Gillespie was the only minister in all Scotland that prayed for Cromwell in his public prayers.[23] Whether the Protestors were consistent in accepting civil and even military support from Cromwell, while denying the right of his authority, is a debatable question. However all through the Commonwealth period they maintained their independence of speech and action; though supported by Cromwell, they were not subservient to him; and when Cromwell forbade the General Assembly to meet, the Protestors did not hesitate to protest publicly against this action.

5.   The Later Covenanters' Estimate of Cromwell.

Covenanters or Reformed Presbyterians since the Revolution of 1688 have unanimously regarded Cromwell as a usurper and a trampler upon the liberties of the Church of Scotland. The Original Judicial Testimony of the Reformed Presbytery (1761) makes the following remarks: "The Lord, then, in his righteous displeasure and controversy with the nation, for betraying of his cause and interest into the hands of his enemies, sold them into the hands of that conquering usurper, Oliver Cromwell, who, having stripped them of their civil liberties, as the most effectual method to rob the church of her spiritual privileges and nullify the forcible obligation of the sacred covenants (which, when preserved, serve as a strong barrier against all such usurpations,) framed a hellish and almost unbounded toleration in Scotland, of heretical and sectarian errors, for gratification of the abettors

---

[22] *Ibid.*, p. 366.

[23] *Ibid.*

thereof, which was followed with a deluge of irreligion and impiety drowning the nation in a still deeper apostacy".[24]

The American Reformed Presbyterian Testimony (1806) is somewhat milder but still speaks of Cromwell as a usurper: "That Cromwell was an usurper, was manifest. He was never chosen by the nation to govern it; and the constitution, ratified by solemn oath, excluded him from power. To this constitution the more faithful Presbyterians considered themselves bound by covenant to adhere".[25]

The Irish Reformed Presbyterian Testimony (1875) speaks more favorably of Cromwell: "The administration of Cromwell, the Lord Protector in Scotland, was on the whole injurious to ministerial freedom, and considerably obstructed the action of the Courts of the Lord's House. Nevertheless we regard it as a matter of devout gratulation that under the countenance and protection extended to the protesters—chiefly because they were believed to be less blindly devoted to the cause of royalty than the Resolutioners—they were kept from being borne down by ecclesiastical opponents, and were for a time preserved as a faithful and powerful protesting party in the land".[26]

The Summary of the Testimony of the Reformed Presbyterian Church of Scotland (1932) makes this statement: "Under Cromwell's rule, public order was strictly maintained in Scotland, and though for several years the Scottish Church was prevented from holding Assemblies, ministers enjoyed

---

[24] *Act, Declaration, and Testimony, for the Whole of our Covenanted Reformation*, etc. Ploughlandhead, Scotland, 1761; Philadelphia, 1876, p.22.

[25] *Reformation Principles Exhibited by the Reformed Presbyterian Church in the United States of America*, New York, 1806; 1919, p. 72.

[26] *Testimony of the Reformed Presbyterian Church of Ireland*, Part II, pp. 74-75.

freedom to preach the Gospel and multitudes were converted".[27]

It is apparent from the above citations that time has considerably modified the Covenanters' estimate of Cromwell's activities. The concensus of opinion would appear to be that Cromwell acted unjustifiably, but that much good resulted from his actions.

6. The Restoration of Charles II, 1660.

Oliver Cromwell died in 1658, on September 3rd, the anniversary of his great victories at Dunbar and Worcester. After his death, the power was held for a time by his son Richard, who, however, lacked his father's ability and force of character. A series of intrigues followed, ending in the Restoration of Charles II. These intrigues were furthered in Scotland by Robert Douglas, one of the leaders of the Resolutioners, and James Sharp, one-time Covenanter who became a persecuting Archbishop after the Restoration. King Charles II was received in London with great festivities on the 29th of May, 1660. He had been an exile from England for ten years.

When Charles II was crowned at Scone on New Year's Day, 1651, he had taken the coronation oath and bound himself to support the National Covenant and the Solemn League and Covenant. When he was restored to the throne of Scotland in 1660, it was done with no conditions or precautions of any kind. The blame for this terrible blunder must be laid chiefly upon the head of James Sharp. Sharp had been sent to London early in 1660 as the agent of a group of Scottish ministers, and he went furnished with detailed

---

[27] *Summary of the Testimony of the Reformed Presbyterian Church of Scotland*, p. 28.

instructions.[28] While in England Sharp betrayed his trust and acted a double part; while posing as the agent of Scottish Presbyterianism he was actually subverting it and plotting for the restoration of Prelacy in Scotland.[29]

After the Restoration, the affairs of the kingdom of Scotland were administered by a council of State, and this council was made up of men known to be opposed to the Covenants and the cause of Presbyterianism.[30]

The Restoration of Charles II marks the end of the Church of Scotland as a covenanted Church, and the beginning of the history of the Covenanters as a dissenting group or party distinct from the judicatories of the Church of Scotland as by law established. The Church of Scotland became officially Episcopalian, and true Presbyterianism could be practiced only in dissenting conventicles and unofficial society meetings, until the Revolution of 1688. After 1688 Presbyterianism was indeed restored by law, but on a somewhat different basis from that of the covenanted Presbyterianism of the period of the Second Reformation.

---

[28] Hetherington, *op. cit.*, pp. 370-371.

[29] *Ibid.*, p. 372.

[30] *Ibid.*, p. 375.

PART II

THE HISTORY OF THE COVENANTERS

CHAPTER I

THE PERIOD OF PERSECUTION, 1660-1688

1. Legal Enactments Affecting the Church of Scotland.

The Earl of Middleton was a Scottish nobleman who had served as an officer both in Covenanting and Royalist armies. After the Restoration, King Charles II appointed him as his Commissioner in Scotland. Middleton called a Parliament, which met on January 1st, 1661, and was later known by the name of the "Drunken Parliament". The members of this Parliament were chiefly persons known to be "Malignant" or opposed to the Covenants, and the Parliament proved to be a very pliable and subservient legislature.[1] The acts passed by this Parliament were an utter subversion of the constitution of the Church and State of Scotland, and had the effect of changing Scotland from a limited to an absolute monarchy.

The first act passed by the Parliament concerned the organization and membership of the Parliament itself, and contained a form of oath of allegiance of a very ensnaring nature. In the title of the act, this form of oath is called "an oath of parliament" but in the body, of the act itself, it is called "an oath of allegiance"; and the form of oath itself was

[1] Johnston, John C., *Treasury of the Scottish Covenant*, p. 122.

in fact an oath of allegiance, with an added sentence to be used when sworn by members of Parliament. The form of oath was as follows: "I, for testification of my faithful obedience to my most gracious and redoubted sovereign Charles, king of Great Britain, France, and Ireland, defender of the faith, do affirm, testify, and declare, by this my solemn oath, that I acknowledge my said sovereign, only supreme governor of this kingdom, over all persons, and in all causes; and that no foreign prince, power, or state, nor person civil or ecclesiastic, hath any jurisdiction, power, or superiority over the same: and therefore I utterly renounce and forsake all foreign jurisdictions, powers, and authorities; and shall at my utmost power defend, assist, and maintain his majesty's jurisdiction foresaid, against all deadly [*sic*], and never decline his majesty's power or jurisdiction, as I shall answer to God". The sentence to be added by members of Parliament was: "And I shall faithfully give my advice and vote in every thing that shall be propounded in parliament, as I shall answer to God".[2]

It will be noted that the teeth in this form of oath are in the words *"over all persons, and in all causes "*. The first phrase, "over all persons", if it meant that all persons in the kingdom were subject to the civil magistrate in civil matters, was quite legitimate and even necessary; but if it meant what Charles II probably meant by it, that the King was supreme above even the Parliament, the courts and the law of the Land, then the phrase was subversive of the civil and religious liberty of the people of Scotland, and utterly contrary to the coronation oath which Charles II had taken at Scone in 1651. But the second phrase was even more subversive; the King was indeed supreme over all persons, if these words were rightly understood; but the King could not be supreme "in all causes" without being supreme in

---

[2] Wodrow, *The History of the Sufferings of the Church of Scotland*, I, p. 92.

ecclesiastical causes as well as in civil. This doctrine of the supremacy of the King in ecclesiastical causes, thus laid down in the form of the oath of allegiance, was the planting of that bitter root of Erastianism which was destined to cause Scotland so much suffering and distress during the years that followed.

Another act of the same Parliament declared that "the king holds his crown from God alone".[3] The Parliament of 1661 thus endeavored to clear the way for the absolutism of Charles II. It was not enough that the King be recognized as the ordinance of God; he must be recognized as the ordinance of God entirely irrespective of the choice of the nation or of his responsibility to the nation.

The crowning piece of legislation enacted by this meeting of Parliament was the Act Rescissory, by which all the acts of Parliaments since the year 1633 were at one stroke repealed.[4] The Act declared all those parliaments to have been "pretendit Parliaments" annulled "all acts and deids past and done in them", declaring these to be "henceforth voyd and null".[5] The effect of this Act was the undoing of all that had been done to make Presbytery the lawful government of the Church of Scotland; this was obviously done in order to clear the way for the reestablishment of Episcopacy and Erastianism. The legal sanction of everything that had been accomplished by the General Assembly of 1638, the Assembly of the Second Reformation, was thus abolished by the "Drunken Parliament".

On December 12th, 1661, the Privy Council issued an order forbidding presentations of candidates for installation

---

[3] *Ibid.*, p. 94.

[4] Johnston, *op. cit.*, p. 123; Wodrow, *op. cit.*, I, p. 101.

[5] Walker, Patrick, *Six Saints of the Covenant*, II, p. 123.

as ministers to be addressed to Presbyteries, and directing Presbyteries not to admit ministers on presentations directed to them.[6]   In January, 1662, the King addressed a letter to the Privy Council in which he forbade all meetings of ecclesiastical judicatories except those held by the Episcopal prelates according to law.[7]   Thus was Presbytery, as a practical system of Church government, outlawed in Scotland.

Parliament met again on May 8th, 1662, and proceeded to make legal provision for the restoration of the prelatic form of Church government in a law entitled "Act for the Restitution and Reestablishment of the Ancient Government of the Church by Archbishops and Bishops",[8] which was passed on May 27th.[9]   The Act Rescissory of 1661 had repealed the acts of all Parliaments held after 1633; the act of May 27th, 1662, went further and repealed the Great Charter of Presbytery of 1592.[10] In the preamble of the act it was stated that it was an inherent right of the crown to order the external polity of the Church, by virtue of the King's supremacy in causes ecclesiastical.[11]

The same meeting of Parliament ratified the appointments of bishops and archbishops which had been made, and invited those prelates, in the King's name, to take seats in Parliament.[12] On June 11th a law was passed which had the most serious consequences for the ministers of

---

[6] Grub, George, *An Ecclesiastical History of Scotland from the Introduction of Christianity to the Present Time*, III, p. 199.

[7] *Ibid.*

[8] Johnston, *op. cit.*, p. 123.

[9] Walker, *op. cit.*, II, p 123; Grub, *op. cit.*, III, pp. 199-200.

[10] Johnston, *op. cit.*, p. 123.

[11] Grub, *op. cit.*, III, pp. 199-200.

[12] *Ibid.*

Scotland. This law declared that all ministers admitted to charges since 1649, when the rights of patrons had been abolished, had no right to their positions, and their parishes were vacant. But every such minister who should obtain a presentation from a patron, before September 20th, 1662, and submit to collation by the bishop of the diocese, should hold his position as if he had been installed in that way at his entry. By the same law the patrons were ordered to grant presentations to ministers, already pastors of Churches, who should apply for the same.[13] This law provided the legal basis for the act of the Privy Council which soon followed and which resulted in hundreds of ministers leaving their Churches for conscience' sake.

By another act of the same Parliament (1662), called the "Abjuration Act", it was declared that "those oaths, the national covenant, as sworn and explained 1638, and afterward, and the solemn league and covenant were, and are in themselves unlawful oaths, and imposed against the fundamental laws of the kingdom".[14] Since Charles II had publicly professed his acceptance of both covenants at his coronation at Scone in 1651, it would appear that the Parliament of 1662 declared that the King himself had taken "unlawful oaths" which were "against the fundamental laws of the kingdom". This Act of Parliament required all persons holding offices of public responsibility in the kingdom to take an oath of abjuration by which entering into covenants, taking arms against the King, the National Covenant and the Solemn League and Covenant were all declared to be unlawfull.[15]

It may be noted at this point that Charles II not only renounced and violated the covenants which he had signed,

---

[13] *Ibid.*

[14] Johnston, *op. cit.*, p. 123; Wodrow, *op. cit.*, I, p. 264.

[15] Grub, *op. cit.*, III, p. 200.

but actually had the offensive documents burned by the common hangman, which was done at London on May 22nd, 1661, and repeated in Scotland at Linlithgow, May 29th, 1662.[16]

Two later legal enactments remain to be mentioned. The first of these was passed November 16th, 1669, and was called the "Assertory Act". This law declared "That his Majesty hath the supreme authority and supremacy over all persons and in all causes ecclesiastical within this his kingdom; and that, by virtue thereof, the ordering and disposal of the external government and policy of the Church doth properly belong to his Majesty and his successors, as an inherent right of the crown; and that his Majesty and his successors may settle, enact, and emit such constitutions, acts, and orders, concerning the administration of the external government of the Church, and the persons employed in the same, and concerning all ecclesiastical meetings, and matters to be proposed and determined therein, as they in their royal wisdom shall think fit".[17] This was Erastianism carried to the utmost extreme; it was too Erastian even for the Episcopal prelates. According to Burnet, the purpose of the act was to enable the King to restore Popery whenever he might choose to do so.[18] This law placed the Church of Scotland so completely in the hands of the King that he could at any time establish any heresy or introduce any corrupt practice, without submitting the matter to Parliament or ecclesiastical courts. Charles II had become a pope as well as a king in Scotland.

---

[16] Johnston, *op. cit.*, p. 122.

[17] *Ibid.*, p. 129; Hetherington,*History of the Church of Scotland*, pp. 429-430.

[18] Hetherington, *op. cit.*, p. 430; Burnet, *History of His Own Times*, I, p. 284.

The other legal enactment which must be mentioned here was the "Test Act" which was passed August 31st, 1681.[19] This law required a special oath of allegiance of every person holding public office. The oath required contains over 500 words and is very complicated. Wodrow calls it "a medley of popery, prelacy, erastianism, and self-contradiction".[20] The person taking this oath must swear that he professes the "true protestant religion, contained in the Confession of Faith, recorded in the first parliament of king James VI" (1567), and at the same time he must swear "that the king's majesty is the only supreme governor of this realm, over all persons, and in all causes, as well ecclesiastical as civil".[21] In this the oath was self-contradictory, because the Confession of Faith referred to taught that Jesus Christ is the only head of the Church so that any person honestly accepting that Confession of Faith could not accept the statement that the king is the supreme governor in ecclesiastical causes. The oath also contained an explicit renunciation of the National Covenant and the Solemn League and Covenant, and a promise never "to endeavour any change or alteration in the government, either in church or state, as it is now established by the laws of this kingdom".[22] About eighty ministers refused to take the "Test" and resigned rather than do so.[23] Even some of the bishops objected to such a contradictory and ensnaring oath, although all of them took it in the end.[24] The Earl of Argyle took the "Test" with an explanation, stating "that he took it in as far as it was consistent with itself, and with the Protestant religion".[25] For

---

[19] Johnston, *op. cit.*, pp. 143-144; Wodrow, *op. cit.*, III, p. 295.

[20] Wodrow, *op. cit.*, III, p. 297.

[21] *Ibid.*, pp. 296-297.

[22] *Ibid.*, p. 297.

[23] Johnston, *op. cit.*, p. 144.

[24] Hetherington, *op. cit.*, p. 480.

[25] *Ibid.*, p. 481.

this he was arrested and tried for treason, and condemned to death. He escaped, however, to Holland, though he was later apprehended and executed in 1685.

2. The Ejection of Ministers, 1662.

The Privy Council met on October 1st, 1662, at Glasgow, and passed an act by which they declared that all of the ministers installed since 1649 who had not yet complied with the law by obtaining presentation by a patron and collation by a bishop, had forfeited their livings, were forbidden to preach, and ordered to remove with their families from the bounds of their parishes before November 1st.[26] According to Burnet, all the members of the Council except Sir James Lockhart were so drunk on that day that they could not consider the matters placed before them.[27]

The order of the Privy Council appears to have been generally obeyed. Patrick Walker, writing after the Revolution, lamented the fact that the ministers were so ready to obey and did not offer more resistance before leaving their pulpits: "Ministers leaving their people, and silence after the unhappy Restoration, was indeed very stumbling and offensive to the Lord's children; and several of these ministers that did so lament it to their dying day, and reckoned it among the causes of God's wrath; as Mr. Shields and others sometimes said on fast-days, that the tout of a horn over the Cross of Edinburgh blew most ministers out of their pulpits." [28]

It has commonly been stated that nearly four hundred ministers were driven from their parishes by the Act of the

---

[26] Grub, *op. cit.*, III, pp. 207-208.

[27] Johnston, *op. cit.*, pp. 124-125.

[28] Walker, *op. cit.*, I, pp. 298-299.

Privy Council.[29]   Wodrow states that nearly one-third of the ministers of Scotland were ejected by the act of the Privy Council, and even more if those forced out by later acts be counted in.[30] Grub, an Episcopalian writer, maintains, however, that this is an exaggeration, and comes to the conclusion that "it is almost certain that the number of those who resigned in the end of the year 1662 fell considerably short even of two hundred".[31] He is inclined to accept Burnet's estimate of 350 as the total number of ministers ejected after the Restoration, including those later ejected for refusing to attend diocesan synods.[32] Grub states that in 1651 there were in Scotland 600 ministers who adhered to the Public Resolutions, and that all except about forty of these accepted Prelacy after the Restoration.[33]

When the Privy Council saw how many ministers had suddenly ceased to officiate, they became alarmed, and on December 23rd, 1662, passed a second act, allowing ministers to apply for presentation and collation up to February 1st, 1663. Under the terms of this act, some who had left their Churches returned and resumed preaching; but when February 1st, 1663, came, many resigned rather than submit. Others were deposed for non-attendance at the diocesan synods. Those who resigned or were ejected included some few of the more distinguished Resolutioners, together with practically all of the Protestors.[34] Those ministers who retained their pulpits were required, of course, to submit to Episcopacy. Since the basic difference between the Resolutioners and the Protestors from the beginning of

---

[29] Johnston, *op. cit.*, pp. 124-125.

[30] Wodrow, *op. cit.* I, p. 283.

[31] Grub, *op. cit.*, III, pp. 209-210.

[32] *Ibid.*

[33] *Ibid.*

[34] *Ibid.*, p. 208.

that controversy had been a difference between political expediency on the one hand and strict adherence to principle on the other, it is not at all surprising that most of the Resolutioners retained their pulpits by conforming to Episcopacy, while nearly all of the Protestors forsook theirs because of their adherence to Presbytery.

3.   Covenanting Conventicles and the Proclamations Issued Against Them.

Many of the ministers who had been ejected in 1662 and 1663 continued to preach, conducting services in private homes and also addressing large audiences in the open fields. These activities naturally displeased both the bishops and the government, and the result was a law passed by Parliament in 1663, entitled "Act for Separation and Disobedience to Ecclesiastic Authority", but popularly known as "The Bishops' Drag-Net".[35]   By the terms of this act, to preach without permission from a bishop was regarded as sedition. Persons who failed to attend the stated services of parish Churches were to be fined. This was the first of a series of measures calculated to force all the people of Scotland into conformity to the established Episcopal Church, and in comparison with what was to follow, it was mild enough. The collection of the fines, and enforcement of Church attendance, were placed in the hands of the military, which was a great grievance to the people. Many of the Episcopal ministers, then popularly called "curates", kept rolls of Church attendance and reported absentees to the soldiers.[36]

In 1664 the Court of High Commission was restored. This Court was not authorized by any law, but was simply a creation of Charles II and depended entirely on the royal

---

[35] Johnston, *op. cit.*, pp. 125-126.

[36] *Ibid.*

prerogative. The Court of High Commission had tremendous power and there was no appeal from its sentence. While this tribunal was set up primarily to persecute the Covenanters, at the beginning it was used principally against the Catholics.[37] The methods used by the Court of High Commission resembled those of the Inquisition. The Court consisted of nine prelates and thirty-five laymen, of whom any five, not less than one being a prelate, constituted a quorum.[38] At this time the Court of High Commission could inflict any punishment short of death; many were fined and imprisoned, others banished, and some sold as slaves.[39] It appears that of all the persons tried by the Court of High Commission, not a single one was acquitted, or escaped without suffering some penalty.[40] The restoration of the Court of High Commission was principally the work of Archbishop Sharp, who felt that the actions of the Privy Council were not sufficient to enforce conformity with Episcopacy in Scotland.

In December, 1665, the Privy Council issued a proclamation against conventicles. According to this proclamation, not only those who preached at conventicles, but also all persons who attended such meetings, were to be regarded as seditious and punished by fines or imprisonment.[41] This measure, however, failed to stop private religious meetings and conventicles; in fact, the conventicles increased rather than diminished.

In the summer of 1670 the Parliament passed a second act against conventicles. All previous measures had failed to stop the "seditious" meetings, and this act, with

---

[37] *Ibid.*, p. 126.

[38] Hetherington, *op. cit.*, p. 407.

[39] *Ibid.*, p. 409; Wodrow, *op. cit.*, I, p. 390.

[40] Hetherington, *op. cit.*, p. 408.

[41] Johnston, *op. cit.*, pp. 126-127.

The Scottish Covenanters

others passed at the same time, provided legislation intended to suppress utterly all religious meetings not held in parish Churches, and to exterminate those who attended and supported such meetings. Every person was required to give evidence on oath concerning conventicles and those who attended them. The penalty for refusal to testify was fine, imprisonment, or banishment.[42] The oath could be administered at any time, and by any public official. All children were to be baptized in the parish Church before the age of thirty days, and any parent unable to produce a satisfactory certificate of baptism after the expiration of that time limit was liable to be fined one-fourth of his annual income.[43] Marriages were to be performed only by the conforming ministers; persons married in any other way were to suffer civil disabilities.[44] This legislation, while intended to suppress conventicles, failed to do so; the effect was rather to force such meetings to be held in greater secrecy and in remoter places than had been done before. One of the most diabolical features of this iniquitous legislation was that it attempted to force persons to give evidence against their most intimate friends and nearest relatives.[45] It is also worthy of note that by this legislation, death and confiscation of goods was the penalty provided for conducting or preaching at a conventicle.[46] Rewards were offered for the capture of conventicle preachers, and if the preacher was killed in the attempt at capture, the would-be captor was promised freedom from prosecution.[47]

In 1676 letters of intercommuning were issued against

---

[42] Hetherington, *op. cit.*, p. 432.

[43] Johnston, *op. cit.*, pp. 129-130.

[44] *Ibid.*

[45] Hetherington, *op. cit.*, p. 432.

[46] *Ibid.*

[47] *Ibid.*

about a hundred persons who had been summoned before the Privy Council but had failed to appear. Those intercommuned were ministers, proprietors of land where conventicles had been held, and other persons.[48] The letters of intercommuning had the effect of making it a crime for any person to hold intercourse- even civil intercourse-with the intercommuned. They were placed outside the pale of society and excluded from the benefits and protection of the law. It was also held a crime to associate in any way with persons who had attended conventicles, and by this ruling it was attempted to cut thousands of Covenanters off from association with their fellow-men.[49] Another outrage was the infliction of fines on the proprietors of lands where conventicles had been held;[50] this was exceedingly unjust as the proprietors might be quite ignorant of the fact of conventicles being held on their estates, and quite helpless to prevent such meetings if they did know about them, for the conventicles were often held in the most remote and inaccessible places.

In April, 1681, a new proclamation against conventicles was issued by the Privy Council in the name of the King. This proclamation ran in part as follows: "Forasmuch as field conventicles, which were in our laws, by the universal consent of all the representatives of this our kingdom, declared to be the rendezvouses of rebellion, are now found, by the undeniable experience of all sober men, to have bred up the unwary commons unto a most atheistical giddiness, to the owning of those murdering principles, which are a reproach to the protestant religion and inconsistent with the security of every private man, and to the contemning of their own masters and landlords: we

---

[48] Johnston, *op. cit.*, p. 131.

[49] *Ibid.*

[50] Hetherington, *op. cit.*, p. 445.

therefore...do hereby command and ordain, that how soon soever any field conventicle, or other conventicles, understood to be field conventicles by construction of law, shall be kept, the heritor in whose lands or house the same is kept...shall immediately advertise the sheriff of the shire...within three days after the same is kept", etc.[51] Persons attending conventicles unarmed were to be dealt with according to the previous legislation for attending conventicles; those who attended armed were to be dealt with for treason.[52]

In 1685, under King James VII (second of England) a Parliament was held by which still more stringent legislation was enacted against the Covenanters. One of the laws passed declared "That the giving or taking the National Covenant or the Solemn League and Covenant, or writing in defence thereof, or owning them as lawful or obligatory upon themselves or others, shall infer the crime and pains of treason".[53] By another act, the death penalty was provided for being present at a conventicle, as well as preaching at one.[54] Even private family worship was treason if more than five non-members of the family were present.[55] During the year 1685 persecution reached its height and many were put to death by soldiers, without process or form of law. Six men were shot on sight at one place, because they were discovered by soldiers while in the act of prayer.[56] The fact or presumption of having been at a conventicle was sufficient ground for instant execution without legal prosecution; ensnaring and contradictory oaths and questions were

---

[51] Wodrow, *op. cit.*, III, pp. 244-245.

[52] *Ibid.*

[53] Hetherington, *op. cit.*, p 505.

[54] *Ibid.*

[55] *Ibid.*

[56] *Ibid.*, p. 503.

proposed to persons apprehended, and in the event of unsatisfactory answers, or refusal to answer, immediate death by shooting was the outcome.[57]

The conventicle movement reached its height in great gatherings at which the Lord's Supper was administered, in 1677 and 1678. One such conventicle was attended by 600 armed men and 7,000 unarmed persons.[58] During the early years of the persecution the conventicles were unarmed gatherings for Presbyterian worship; as the laws and regulations against such meetings became more stringent, and were more rigorously enforced, the Covenanters adopted the practice of attending conventicles armed for the purpose of self-defence. They would not use arms to propagate their religion, but only to defend it, and in this they were able to find sufficient warrant for their course in the Bible itself. Their principle was that they ought to obey God rather than men.

4.   The Indulgences and the Covenanters' Attitude Toward Them.

During the period of persecution between the Restoration and the Revolution, King Charles II issued three and King James VII four "Indulgences". These were royal offers to permit some of the ejected ministers to resume their ministry under certain regulations.

The first Indulgence of Charles II was proclaimed in 1669. On July 15th of that year, a letter from the King to the Privy Council directed the Council to "appoint so many of the ejected ministers as had lived peaceably and orderly",[59] to

---

[57] *Ibid.*, p.502.

[58] Johnston, *op. cit.*, pp. 147-148; cf. Blackadder, *Memoirs*, p. 145; Gilfillan, *Martyrs and Heroes*, p. 78.

[59] Hetherington, *op. cit.*, pp. 426-427.

return to their original parishes, or to others if those were no longer vacant. Those accepting the Indulgence had, in order to claim the stipend of the parish, to obtain presentation from the patron and collation from the bishop of the diocese. If unwilling to submit to these requirements, they could exercise their ministry and have the use of the manse and glebe. Other conditions attached to this Indulgence were that those who accepted it must attend the prelatic diocesan synods, must not permit people from other parishes to attend their preaching or receive ordinances from them, and must not publicly speak or preach against the doctrine that the king is supreme in all ecclesiastical causes.[60]

This Indulgence was not offered to all the ejected ministers, but only to a favored few, most of whom were Resolutioners. It was first offered to ten ministers and later to a larger number.[61] In the end about forty accepted it,[62] and all of them made some kind of a qualifying statement concerning their understanding of the King's supremacy over the Church.[63] Some of them stated, "We having received our ministry from Jesus Christ, with prescriptions from Him regulating us therein, must, in the discharge thereof, be accountable to Him".[64] Although forty or more ministers accepted the first Indulgence, few of them sought presentation by patrons or collation by bishops.[65] This fact shows that their conduct, while it must be regarded as a sacrifice of principle, proceeded from unselfish motives; they were willing to give up their stipends if only they could exercise the functions of the ministry in peace. Even so,

[60] Ibid.; Johnston, *op. cit*, pp. 127-129.

[61] Hetherington. *op. cit.*, pp. 427-428.

[62] *Ibid.*, pp. 428-429; Johnston, *op cit.*, pp 127-129.

[63] Hetherington, *op. cit.*, pp. 428-429.

[64] *Ibid.*, pp. 427-428.

[65] *Ibid.*, pp. 428-429.

however, they compromised with prelacy.

The effect of the first and all following Indulgences was to weaken the Covenanters' cause by driving a wedge of division into their ranks. From 1669 on the ministers of Scotland were divided into the Indulged and the Non-indulged. Concerning the propriety of accepting the Indulgence, a great deal has been written. Hetherington says that "the whole discussion may be resolved into the question, which of three things ought to have been chosen by the Church; whether unanimously to accept the Indulgence, in which case she would at once have become prelatic; or unanimously to reject it, in which case it would fall harmlessly to the ground; or some to receive and some to reject, in which case the Church would be divided, weakened, and trampled in the dust. The first could not be chosen without perjury; the second would have been the choice of high principles and sound prudence; the third was the course followed, recommended by the usual weak and short-sighted arguments of expediency, and proved to be the course of ruin".[66] It will be noted that the terms on which part of the ejected ministers were offered back their pulpits were practically the same as the terms on which they might have retained them in 1662. The Indulgence, then, instead of being a concession of anything by the King, was simply one more chance for Presbyterian ministers to keep their pulpits and their livings by becoming Episcopalians. If it is right for a covenanted Presbyterian to become an Episcopalian in order to keep the door open for preaching, then it was right to accept the first Indulgence. On the other hand if becoming Episcopalians involved a sacrifice of principle and a compromise with an unscriptural form of Church government, then it was wrong to accept the first Indulgence, and no reasons of expediency could justify the acceptance of

---

[66] *Ibid.*

it. But even outweighing the fact that acceptance of the Indulgence meant conforming to Episcopacy, was the fact that it meant conforming to Erastianism in its most extreme form. The Indulgence proceeded from the King's alleged supremacy over the Church; to accept the Indulgence meant to accept that Erastian supremacy, and this acceptance was not merely implied in accepting the Indulgence, but it was actually one of the stated conditions attached to the offer, for the Indulged ministers were warned against preaching or speaking against the King's supremacy in causes ecclesiastical.

In 1670 an attempt was made by the government to bring about an agreement between Presbyterians and Episcopalians in Scotland. Robert Leighton, one of the Scottish bishops appointed by Charles II, with the approval of the government, selected six of the Episcopal ministers, and accompanied by these travelled over the western counties of Scotland, attempting to win the people over to conformity to Episcopacy. Leighton was a good man and one who was grieved by the worldliness and abuses which existed among the prelatic clergy. Gilbert Burnet, then professor of theology in Glasgow University, was one of the ministers who accompanied Leighton, and he has left us an interesting account of the people's reaction to the attempt to win them over. "The people of the country", he writes, "came generally to hear us, though not in great crowds. We were indeed amazed to see a poor commonalty so capable to argue upon points of government, and on the bounds to be set to the power of princes in matters of religion: upon all these topics they had texts of Scripture at hand, and were ready with their answers to anything that was said to them. This measure of knowledge was spread even among the meanest of them, their cottagers and their servants... The ministers had brought the people to such a degree of knowledge that cottagers and servants would have prayed *extempore*. I have often heard them at it; and, though there was a large mixture of odd stuff, yet I have been astonished to hear how copious and ready they were in it".[67] This attempt to win the people over to Episcopacy was called the "Accommodation". Conferences were held in various places, but the whole attempt failed. The strict Covenanters knew their Bibles and their Church polity too well, and saw altogether too clearly the principles at stake, to yield to any such attempt.

The second Indulgence of Charles II was announced on September 3rd, 1672.[68] It was offered to some eighty previously non-indulged ministers, many of whom rejected the offer.[69] By the terms of this Indulgence, those who accepted it were placed two by two as joint pastors with each other or with previously indulged ministers.[70] The object of this arrangement was apparently to confine the hitherto nonconforming ministers in the smallest possible bounds and thus limit their influence. They were forbidden to preach except in their own parishes,[71] and were hemmed in by the same Erastian regulations as those who had accepted the first Indulgence. Although many rejected the second Indulgence, some accepted it, driving the wedge of division deeper into the ranks of the Covenanters. When the offer was proposed to a Mr. Blair, minister of Galston, he received the paper from the official who offered it, saying, "My Lord Chancellor, I cannot be so uncivil as to refuse a paper offered to me by your Lordship". He then let the paper fall to the floor, and added, "but I can receive no instructions from you for regulating the exercise of my ministry; for if I should

---

[67] Johnston, *op. cit.*, p. 130; Cf. Burnet, *op. cit.*, I, p. 293.

[68] Hetherington, *op cit.*, pp. 437-438.

[69] Johnston, *op. cit.*, pp 127-129.

[70] Hetherington, *op cit.*, pp. 437-438.

[71] *Ibid.*

receive instructions from you, I should be your ambassador, not Christ's".[72] This action caused great excitement; many ministers condemned Blair, while others defended his action. Blair himself was imprisoned for his words, and died soon after.[73]

Patrick Walker's comment on those who accepted the first and second Indulgences of Charles II is straightforward and to the point: "Headlong they went to the unfathomable depth of defection, in their embracing of the Christ-dethroning, church-ruining, remnant-renting, zeal-quenching indulgence; where they lay in that puddle, with foul hands and garments, the first of them for 18 years, and the second for 11 years,[74] juggling and dissembling...".[75] Patrick Walker was not a man to smooth over an ugly matter with sweet and pleasant words; we can imagine what he would have said about such a document as the *Auburn Affirmation*.

The third Indulgence of Charles II was proclaimed on June 29th, 1679, a few days after the battle of Bothwell Bridge, in the form of "A proclamation suspending laws against conventicles".[76] Like the former Indulgences, this one assumed the supremacy of the King in causes ecclesiastical. It suspended the execution of the laws against house conventicles, under certain regulations and restrictions, and specifically excepted a zone of two miles around Edinburgh and one mile around certain other places, the King "being fully resolved, not to suffer the seat of our government, nor our universities to be pestered with any irregularities

---

[72] *Ibid.*, pp 438-439.

[73] *Ibid.*

[74] This statement is a mistake. From the second Indulgence to the Revolution was sixteen years, not eleven years.

[75] Walker, *op. cit.*, I, p. 348.

[76] Wodrow, *op. cit.*, III, p. 149.

whatsoever".[77] The Indulgence did not permit open air or field meetings, and it also specifically excepted those who had been involved in the "late rebellion" (Bothwell). As in the case of the former Indulgences, some accepted the third Indulgence and some rejected it. Under its terms, some ministers were released from prison.[78] Altogether some fifteen ministers resumed preaching on account of the third Indulgence.[79] But the toleration granted was of short duration; in a short time Erastian suppression and persecution were resumed.[80]

In 1685 Charles II died and James VII (II of England) became King. James, formerly the Duke of York, was a Roman Catholic, and during his brief reign persecution of the strict Covenanters who kept field meetings reached its bitterest extreme, so that the years from 1685 to 1688 have been known as "the Killing time". King James VII issued four Indulgences, the first of which, intended for the benefit of Roman Catholics, was proclaimed on February 12th, 1687 in a letter from the King to the Privy Council, in which the King "by his sovereign authority, prerogative royal, and absolute power, which all his subjects are to obey without reserve" granted his "royal toleration to the several professors of Christian religion".[81] The proclamation continues: "In the first place, we allow and tolerate the *moderate* Presbyterians to meet in their private houses, and there to hear all such ministers as either have, or are willing to accept of our Indulgence, and none other".[82] The laws against field

---

[77] *Ibid.*

[78] Hewison, James King, *The Covenanters: History of the Church of Scotland from the Reformation to the Revolution*, II, p. 321.

[79] *Ibid.*

[80] Smellie, Alexander, *Men of the Covenant*, p. 373.

[81] Hetherington, *op. cit.*, p. 520.

[82] *Ibid.*

conventicles were to remain in full force. The main purpose of the proclamation is then stated: the King by the royal prerogative and absolute power annulled all laws against Roman Catholics, gave them freedom of worship, made them eligible for public office, and abolished the Test, providing instead a new form of oath of allegiance owning the absolute power of the King.[83] Like the Indulgences of Charles II, this one was thoroughly Erastian in nature and proceeded from the alleged supremacy of the King in causes ecclesiastical. It satisfied none but the Roman Catholics. The strict Covenanters continued their field conventicles and ignored the King's proposal.[84] Patrick Walker says of the first Indulgence of King James VII, "The very design of that Popish toleration 1687, was, to lull all asleep, that they might get their bloody designs effectuate in a massacre; which were all stopt and crusht of their desires and designs, by the very remarkable steps of the Lord's providence".[85] There seems to be general agreement, at any rate, that this Indulgence was intended to help the Catholics, and that the Presbyterians were included for the sake of appearances rather than from any real intention to help them.

The second Indulgence of King James VII followed soon after the first, on March 31st, 1687. This proclamation authorized the Privy Council to omit the oath and allow Presbyterian ministers to conduct services in private houses. Some ministers preached in houses, but not because of the Indulgence, and this was reported to the King by the Privy Council as the submission of all the ministers.[86] The third Indulgence of James VII was proclaimed at Edinburgh on the 5th of July, 1687. In this the King "by his sovereign

---

[83] Wodrow, *op. cit.*, IV, pp. 417-419.

[84] Hetherington, *op. cit.*, pp. 520-521.

[85] Walker, *op. cit.*, I, p. 7.

[86] Hetherington, *op. cit.*, p. 521.

authority, prerogative royal, and absolute power" suspended all laws against non-conformity in religion, and permitted Presbyterians "to meet and serve God after their own way and manner, be it in private houses, chapels, or places purposely hired or built for that use, so that they take care that nothing be preached or taught among them which may any ways tend to alienate the hearts of our people from us or our government".[87] The laws against field conventicles were left "in full force and vigour",[88] as the King held that, after this Indulgence, there could be no excuse for field meetings. This Indulgence was accepted by nearly all Presbyterian ministers in Scotland, except the strict covenanters, who had just published their "Informatory Vindication", a statement and defence of their principles. They consistently rejected not only all of the Indulgences, but the very idea that an inalienable human right, the right to worship God according to his revealed will, can be either tolerated or restricted by any earthly ruler. An earthly king might *recognize* the right of his subjects to worship God according to the Scriptural pattern, but he could not lawfully *tolerate* such a right, for the very idea of toleration implies that the thing in question is not a right but a privilege that may be granted or withheld at pleasure. What the strict Covenanters saw clearly was, that the whole series of Indulgences was in essence not a recognition of man's right to worship God according to Scripture, but a mere concession or granting of privilege, which proceeded wholly from the utterly vicious doctrine of the supremacy of the King in causes ecclesiastical. The Covenanters saw that the Indulgences were Erastian to the core and utterly opposed to divine law and human freedom, and they held aloof from the whole system as from an unclean thing. To the bitter end they rejected every offer of Erastian toleration, maintained their high principle of the sole

---

[87] *Ibid.* pp. 521-522.

[88] *Ibid.*

headship of Christ over the Church, and continued their field meetings.

From the time of the first Indulgence of Charles II, 1669, many Covenanting ministers preached against the Indulgence, but their preaching of *separation from the indulged* did not begin until much later; Patrick Walker says that it began in 1677.[89] Wodrow states that Richard Cameron was the first minister to preach separation from the indulged ministers,[90] but Patrick Walker states that this is contrary to fact, because John Welwood, John Kid and others did the same before Cameron, whose preaching was during 1680.[91] Walker quotes the following from a sermon by Kid, preached before Cameron preached separation from the indulged: "There is not a clean pulpit in all Scotland this day, curate nor indulged; wherefore come out among them, and be ye separate, saith the Lord, and touch not these unclean things, and I will be a father unto you, and ye shall be my sons and daughters, saith the Lord Almighty".[92]

On May 15th, 1688, King James VII issued a fourth and final Indulgence. This Indulgence reaffirms the former ones, and like them speaks of the King's "sovereign authority, prerogative royal, and absolute power" which it states were "so plainly acknowledged by several acts of parliament".[93] The Indulgence abolishes all oaths and religious tests for public office, and proclaims freedom of religion to all subjects. While this Indulgence was in some ways an improvement over the former ones, still it was vitiated by the fact that it proceeded from the absolute power

---

[89] Walker, *op. cit.*, I, p. 308.

[90] Wodrow, *op. cit.*, III, p. 220.

[91] Walker, *op. cit.*, I, pp. 333-334.

[92] *Ibid.*

[93] Wodrow, *op cit.*, IV, p. 440.

of the monarch. The strict Covenanters, who had held themselves aloof from all the Indulgences, were on principle opposed to this one as to the former ones, not only because it proceeded from the King's "absolute power" but because the King was a Roman Catholic and therefore in their judgment had no right to the throne of Scotland, and because the fourth Indulgence tolerated not merely Presbyterianism but Roman Catholicism as well. Still the fourth Indulgence of James VII was the beginning of the end of persecution of the Covenanters. James Renwick had been hanged in February, 1688; the last Covenanter martyr, George Wood, a boy of sixteen years, was shot on sight during July (?) 1688.[94] The persecuted Covenanters, followers of Cameron, Cargill and Renwick, had scorned seven Erastian Indulgences and had maintained pure Presbyterian worship in spite of all the opposition of the civil and military power of the land, for nearly thirty years.

5.   The Covenanters' Attempts at Armed Resistance.

Early in 1666 Sir James Turner was sent with a body of troops to police the south and west of Scotland and keep the "Whigs", as the Covenanters were called, under control. Turner and his men enforced the law against conventicles, and exacted unreasonable and oppressive fines from the people. In November of that year, some of Turner's men arrested an old farmer named Grier, for failure to pay the fine for absence from the parish Church. The soldiers bound Grier hand and foot, and threatened to strip him naked and roast him on a hot gridiron because of the unpaid fine.[95] Four Covenanters heard of this, and went and rescued Grier, disarming his captors. Realizing, apparently, that if

---

[94] Hewison, *op. cit.*, II, p. 512.

[95] *Ibid.*, II, p. 191.

apprehended they would be held guilty of rebellion, they determined to make a stand in defence of their rights and liberties, and the next morning attacked and overcame a party of about a dozen soldiers, one of whom was killed in the fight, and the rest taken prisoners.[96] After this a number of the local gentry joined the little band of Covenanters and together they marched to the town of Dumfries and captured their persecutor, Sir James Turner. Their idea apparently was that with Turner in their hands they could be sure of a hearing from the government.[97] After capturing Turner, they went to the market place of Dumfries, where they publicly proclaimed their object to be simply self-defence. After this they drank the King's health,"[98] and pledged their loyalty to the government of Charles II. Turner was treated kindly, although he had been a great persecutor of the Covenanters. When it was proposed to shoot him, one of the Covenanters, named Neilson, whose property had been much damaged by Turner's soldiers, opposed this so firmly that the idea was dropped.[99] From Dumfries they marched, seven hundred strong,[100] to Lanark, where they formally renewed the Solemn League and Covenant, and also issued a declaration stating their reasons for appearing in arms, which were self-defence, maintenance of the Covenant, and protest against the apostasy and cruelties of the times.[101]

The insurgent Covenanters, now numbering over a thousand men,[102] marched towards Edinburgh, led by Colonel James Wallace. At Rullion Green in the Pentland hills they

[96] Hetherington, *op. cit.*, p. 411.

[97] Hewison, *op. cit*, II, p. 192.

[98] *Ibid.*, II, p. 193; Hetherington, *op. cit.*, p. 411.

[99] Hewison, *op. cit.*, II, p. 195; Hetherington, *op. cit.*, p. 412.

[100] Smellie, *op. cit.*, p. 163.

[101] Hewison, *op. cit.*, II, p. 195; Hetherington, *op cit.*, pp. 413-414.

[102] Smellie, *op. cit.*, p. 163.

were opposed by the King's troops and the battle was drawn. The Covenanters at this time had nine hundred men, and the King's forces under Dalziel between two and three thousand soldiers.[103] It was a hard fight, but the Covenanters were hopelessly out numbered, and suffered complete defeat. Of their nine hundred men, forty or fifty were killed in the battle, and seventy or eighty captured, and the remaining seven or eight hundred took advantage of the semi-darkness of the evening, and escaped to the hills.[104]

Of those captured at Rullion Green, some twenty were found guilty of rebellion and executed by hanging.[105] The authorities believed that the Pentland rising must have been the result of a well developed plot, and in order to obtain evidence of this, put some of the captives to the torture of the "boot", by which the bones of the leg were mashed to pulp. But even when tortured, the captured Covenanters did not reveal any plot against the government, and the verdict of history is that no such plot existed. The Pentland rising was a desperate, but entirely spontaneous and unpremeditated, attempt at self-defence on the part of people who had been vexed beyond the breaking point by their oppressors.

Nearly thirteen years passed before another armed conflict took place between the Covenanters and the King's forces. On May 3rd, 1679, Archbishop Sharp, one of the chief persecutors, was overtaken in his carriage on Magus Moor, near St. Andrews, by a group of Covenanters and immediately assassinated. Although extenuating circumstances existed, it is impossible to justify this deed of blood, and as a matter of fact very few Covenanters justified it at the time or afterwards. Many who had nothing to do with the

---

[103] Hetherington, *op. cit.*, p. 415.

[104] Smellie, *op. cit.*, p. 166.

[105] Wodrow, *op. cit.*, II, pp 48, 49-50, 52-53.

assassination of the Archbishop were later interrogated by the
authorities, and when asked whether the killing of the
Archbishop was murder refuse to commit themselves, not
because they wished to justify the deed, but because they did
not believe it their duty to pass judgment on a matter with
which they had no connection and concerning which they
were not in possession of all the facts. Later in May, 1679, a
proclamation against field conventicles was issued, in which
they were called "rendezvouses of rebellion", and all who
went to armed conventicles were declared to be guilty of
treason.[106] On May 29th a party of Covenanters published the
Rutherglen declaration, a statement of their principles and a
condemnation of the defections of the land. The Rutherglen
declaration was declared to be rebellion, and the government
set about apprehending those responsible for it. The
Covenanters resolved to defend themselves if possible. A
body of somewhat less than two hundred of them prepared to
fight at a swampy place called Drumclog.[107] Claverhouse, in
command of the King's troops, approached and attacked
them, but suffered defeat at the hands of the Covenanters.
Five of the King's soldiers were captured, and over thirty
killed.[108]

The Covenanters who fought at Drumclog resolved to
remain together for mutual self-defence. Soon large numbers
of like-minded persons joined them, and it was thought
proper to publish a statement of their reasons for being in
arms. When they began to discuss the proposed statement
dissensions broke out among them. Part of them wished to
include a pledge of loyalty to Charles II, and part opposed
this because of the King's violation of the Covenants. Part
wished to put the whole body on record as being opposed to

[106] Hetherington, *op. cit.*, pp. 457-458.
[107] *Ibid.*, p. 459.
[108] *Ibid.*, p. 460.

the Indulgence, and part opposed this because unwilling to go to the length of complete separation from the indulged ministers.[109] Before their dissensions were settled, they were attacked on the Sabbath morning, June 22nd, 1679, by the King's forces at Bothwell, where the Covenanters were in possession of the bridge. They defended the bridge as long as their ammunition lasted, and then gave way. They suffered a disastrous rout; in addition to those killed in the battle, some four hundred were killed while attempting to escape, and twelve hundred in one body surrendered to the royal troops.[110]

The prisoners taken after the battle at Bothwell were removed to Edinburgh and confined for five months in the Greyfriars' churchyard in a miserable condition.[111] The uprising was officially declared to have been rebellion and those involved in it to be traitors.[112] The prisoners were given an opportunity to regain their freedom by signing a bond in which they called the uprising "rebellion" and promised not to take up arms against the King's forces. Some signed this bond but others would not call the insurrection "rebellion" nor promise not to take up arms in self-defence. Two hundred and fifty of the latter were ordered transported to Barbadoes to be sold as slaves, but the ship was wrecked and all were drowned except about fifty who escaped alive.[113]

The publication of the Sanquhar Declaration by the strict Covenanters, under the leadership of Richard Cameron, on June 22nd, 1680, brought great wrath upon the desperate men who had thus deliberately published their principles to

[109] M'Crie, Thomas, *Sketches of Scottish Church History*, II, pp. 171-173.
[110] Hetherington, *op. cit.*, pp. 463-464; Wodrow, *op. cit.*, III, pp. 88-110.
[111] Hetherington, *op. cit.*, p. 465.
[112] *Ibid.*
[113] *Ibid.*

the world. Just a month after the posting of the Sanquhar Declaration, on July 22nd, a party of sixty-three Covenanters, including Cameron, was attacked by the King's forces. They determined to do what they could to defend themselves, and although but poorly armed, prepared to resist the attack. Cameron offered prayer, committing the matter to God, and using the expression, "Lord, spare the green, and take the ripe".[114] The Covenanters fought bravely, and killed twenty-eight of the King's soldiers; nine Covenanters, including Cameron, were killed in the skirmish, and the rest taken prisoners, of whom several died of wounds within the next few days.[115] The soldiers cut off Cameron's head and hands, to send them to Edinburgh, one of them saying "These are the head and hands of a man who lived preaching and praying, and died fighting and praying".[116] This conflict took place at a place called Ayrsmoss, and was the last armed conflict between an organized body of Covenanters and the King's forces.

Covenanters in later times have always regarded these attempts at armed resistance as legitimate and righteous self-defence. The Testimony of the Reformed Presbyterian Church of Ireland speaks thus of them: "The appearance in arms at Pentland, Drumclog, Bothwell-Bridge, and Airsmoss in unpremeditated attempts at necessary, though desperate self-defence, and in vindication of the outraged liberties of the church and nation, we regard as justifiable on the admitted principles of national law, from the examples of God's saints recorded in history, and the noble struggles of such nations as have achieved constitutional freedom. To some, indeed, they may appear to have been rash and inexpedient, inasmuch as they led to increased sufferings and oppression. They

---

[114] *Ibid.*, p. 472.

[115] *Ibid.*

[116] *Ibid.*

served, nevertheless, as a just though unsuccessful protest against the reckless conduct of infatuated rulers, and as an impressive testimony in behalf of principles which the British nation endorsed in the ultimate rejection of the house of Stuart".[117]

6. Public Protests and Testimonies Issued by the Covenanters.

In May, 1679, the government had issued a proclamation calling the field conventicles "rendezvouses of rebellion" and declaring that all who attended them were traitors. This act of the government was the occasion for the publication of the Rutherglen Testimony, on May 29th, 1679. The strict Covenanters decided it was time to publish their principles to the world, and selected Thomas Douglas, a minister, and Robert Hamilton, brother of the laird of Preston, to go with eighty armed men to the town of Rutherglen for this purpose. The little band assembled at the market cross of Rutherglen, where they burned certain acts and papers, and published a declaration, which they also affixed to the cross. The declaration was entitled "The Declaration and Testimony of Some of the True Presbyterian Party in Scotland".[118] The Rutherglen Testimony was a condemnation of various laws enacted since the Restoration, including (1) The Act Rescissory; (2) The acts re-establishing Prelacy; (3) The requirement that persons holding public office renounce the Covenants; (4) The act which resulted in the ejection of ministers in 1662; (5) The act requiring the anniversary of the Restoration to be kept as a holiday; (6) The Assertory Act of 1669 which declared that the King is supreme in all causes ecclesiastical. In addition to these, the Testimony condemned all Acts of Council for enforcing the

---

[117] *Testimony of the Reformed Presbyterian Church of Ireland*, Part II, (Historical), p. 89.

[118] Johnston, *op. cit.*, pp. 131-132.

King's supremacy over the Church. The document was unsigned.[119]

During the interval between the publication of the Rutherglen Testimony and the battle of Bothwell Bridge, there was much controversy among the Covenanters as they endeavored to formulate a statement of their reasons for being in arms. Finally after much debate a statement was adopted by them, which was published at the cross of Glasgow, June 13th, 1679. It appears that this paper was not satisfactory to the strict Covenanters, who later became the Cameronians. Wodrow tells us that although none of these disowned the paper at the time, some "highly complained of" it.[120] Some of them later claimed that John Welsh and David Hume had made the paper public at Glasgow "Against faith and promise".[121] Some of the martyrs in their final testimonies explicitly disowned the document and listed it as a defection.[122] Robert Gray, who was executed in 1682, said of it in his dying testimony, "I also adhere to and heartily join with the Rutherglen Declaration; and I disown the Hamilton Declaration, because it took in the malignant interest".[123] The paper, which was later printed and circulated by Welsh and Hume, was a reasoned defence of the conduct of the Covenanters in resorting to the use of arms in self-defence.[124] It enumerated three causes for their action, as follows: "1st. The defending and securing of the true protestant religion, and presbyterian government founded on the word of God, and summarily comprehended in our confessions of faith and catechisms, and established by the laws of this land, to which

[119] *Ibid.*

[120] Wodrow, *op. cit.*, III, p. 95.

[121] *Ibid.*, p. 94.

[122] *Ibid.*, p. 95.

[123] *A Cloud of Witnesses for the Royal Prerogatives of Jesus Christ*, p, 233.

[124] Johnston, *op. cit.*, pp. 132-134; Wodrow, *op. cit.*, III, pp.94-95.

king, nobles and people are solemnly sworn, and engaged in our national and solemn league and covenants, and more particularly the defending and maintaining of the kingly authority of our Lord Jesus Christ over his Church against all sinful supremacy, derogatory thereto, and encroaching thereupon. 2ndly.The preserving and defending the king's majesty's person and authority in the preservation and defence of the true religion and liberties of the kingdom, that the world may bear witness, with our consciences, of our loyalty, and that we have no thoughts nor intentions to diminish his just power and greatness. 3rdly. The obtaining of a free and unlimited parliament, and of a free general assembly, in order to the redressing of our foresaid grievances, for preventing the danger of popery, and extirpation of prelacy".[125] The paper concluded with a petition to the King for redress of grievances: "We humbly request the king's majesty would restore all things as he found them, when God brought him home to his crown and kingdoms; and if that cannot be obtained, then we heartily and humbly invite, intreat, beseech, and obtest, in the bowels of Jesus Christ, all who are under the same bonds with us, to concur in the defence of this common cause and interest, and that they would not stand still, and see, not only us oppressed, but this foresaid cause ruined, adversaries highly and proudly insult against God and all good men, friends of the truth discouraged, yea, the protestant cause in Britain and Ireland, and even yourselves, within a little time, made a prey of, or else forced, when we are broken, (which the good Lord prevent) dreadfully to wrong your consciences. Finally. Because we desire no man's hurt nor blood, we request our countrymen, now the standing forces of this kingdom, some of them being our friends and kinsmen, not to fight against us, lest in so doing they be found fighting against the Lord, whose cause and quarrel we are sure he will own and signally

---

[125] Wodrow, *op. cit*, III, p. 95.

countenance, seeing we fight under his banner who is the Lord of hosts".[126]

It was the recognition of the authority of the King in this paper which caused the strict Covenanters to complain against it, and later repudiate it. Their contention was that Charles II had forfeited his right to the throne by his repudiation of the Covenants which amounted to a repudiation of the coronation oath by which he had obtained the crown at Scone in 1651. The majority prevailed, however, and the "king's interest" was included in the paper, and no Covenanter publicly disowned it at the time. This paper, then, marks the time when the Covenanters, though still maintaining their unity, were on the point of dividing into two groups on the question of allegiance to Charles II. As time went on, and as the suppression of conventicles proceeded with increasing rigor, those who favored the position taken in the Glasgow paper of June 13th, 1679, ceased to be vocal, and either took advantage of the Indulgences, or retired into isolated silence, neither complying with the defections of the times, nor identifying themselves with public protests against them. The other group, which in 1679 was too small a minority to prevent the adoption of the Glasgow paper, continued to hold field conventicles and to protest against the evils which they opposed, throughout the period of persecution and down to the Revolution of 1688.

On June 4th, 1680, a paper was found on the person of Henry Hall, a strict Covenanter who was apprehended at South Queensferry, from which fact the paper was afterwards known as the Queensferry Paper. It was an unsigned document, but is regarded as having been produced by the

---

[126] *Ibid.*

joint labors of Hall and Donald Cargill.[127]   The document was long, comprising about 6,000 words. As it was the first formal statement of the distinctive principles of the group which later became known as Cameronians, MacMillanites and Reformed Presbyterians, it may be worth while to give here a summary of its contents.

It begins with a statement of purpose. "...And as we resolve to covenant with and before God, so to declare before the world, what are the designs we propose to pursue, if God shall give us power and success, that men (knowing) if they will know, our inward thoughts and utmost end, and our way from the one to the other, may not be at a trouble or uncertainty to find us out, and may have no occasion to misjudge, nor misrepute us that are friends, and those that have the glory of God before their eyes (as we may have no cause to be jealous of our intentions) and that our enemies with their associate backsliders (sometime professed friends) may not have ground to load us with foul and odious aspersions, but that all knowing the truth of things, those who oppose the kingdom of God with us may do it without excuse, and those who join with us may do it on solid grounds, and in hazarding their perishing lives, may know they do not die as fools". The paper then lists the principles for which the writers stand: (1) Acknowledgement of the Trinity; the way of redemption by Jesus Christ; His righteousness as that only whereby a man can be justified before God; the authority and inspiration of the Scriptures; the Scriptures the only rule of faith and life; self-dedication to God to live according to his word and by his Spirit. (2) Profession of intention to advance the kingdom of God by establishing the true Reformed religion, in the truth of its doctrine, purity and power of its worship and ordinances, its right government and discipline, and to free the Church of

---

[127] Johnston, *op. cit.*, pp 134-141.

God from the tyranny and corruption of Prelacy on the one hand, and the thraldom and encroachments of Erastianism of the other hand; "and that we shall, to the utmost of our power, relieve the Church and our brethren, the subjects of this kingdom (God authorising and calling us to this by His raising us up, and giving us power and success in removing those who by their transgression have forfeited their authority) of that oppression that hath been exercised upon their consciences, civil rights and liberties, that men may serve God holily without fear, and posess their civil rights peaceably without disturbance". (3) Acknowledgement of the doctrine of the Reformed Churches, especially that of Scotland, contained in the Scriptures, summed up in the Confessions of Faith and Covenants: of the pure worship required and prescribed in the Scriptures without the inventions, additions, adornings, or corruptions of man, as the only true worship of God; acknowledgement of the Presbyterian system of church government as the only right government of the Church, distinct from the civil government, and to be distinctly exercised, "not after a carnal manner by the plurality of votes, or authority of a single person, but according to the Word of God; so that the Word makes and carries the sentence, and not plurality of votes". (4) Endeavor to overthrow the kingdom of darkness, especially idolatry, popery, superstition, will-worship and Prelacy with its hierarchy; "and that we shall with the same sincerity endeavour the overthrow of that power (it being no more authority) that hath established, and upholds that kingdom of darkness, that Prelacy, to wit, and Erastianism over the Church, and hath exercised such a lustful and arbitrary tyranny over the subjects, taken all power in their hand, that they may at their pleasure introduce Popery in the Church, as they have done arbitrary government in the state...". (5) Here follows a long list of the sins and crimes of the House of Stuart, and a declaration that they are no longer governors, but "a lustful rage", "which all ought to set themselves against, as they would do against pestilence, sword, and famine raging among them". In a sub-heading of point 5 three questions are raised and answered: first, "Whether the deed and obligation of our ancestors can bind us" (i.e., in allegiance to the Stuarts); this is answered in the negative: "Neither did they bind us to anything but to a government, which they then esteemed the best for the commonwealth and subjects; and when this ceaseth we are free to choose another, if we see it more conducible for that end, and more free of these inconveniences". Second, "Whether the Covenant doth bind us either to this man or to his posterity"; this is also answered in the negative: "The Covenant doth not, for it only binds us to maintain our king in the maintenance of the true established and covenanted religion; and this we have not: neither can they require homage upon the account of the Covenant, having renounced and disclaimed that Covenant: and we being no otherwise bound, the Covenant being the coronation compact, without the swearing and sealing of which our fathers, or rather we ourselves, refused to receive him for king, and them for rulers; and if they were free to refuse him for king upon the account of not subscribing of that Covenant, we are much more free to reject him upon his renouncing of it, this being the only way of receiving the crown of Scotland; and reigning also, not being an inheritance that passes from father to son without the consent of tenants, but an (and the more men plead for this, the more we are concerned to look to it) office, which, all say, is given *ad culpam, non ad vitam* ." Third, "Whether there is yet any hope of them and their posterity". This also is answered in the negative, on the ground that the Stuarts had hypocritically repented many times already. Point 5 continues, "...we then upon these and the following grounds, do reject that king, and those associate with him in the government (stated and declared enemies to Jesus Christ) from being our king and rulers, because standing in the way of our right, free, and peaceable serving of God, propagating His kingdom and Reformation, and overthrowing Satan's kingdom, according to our Covenants, declare them to be henceforth no lawful rulers, as they have declared us to be no lawful subjects, upon a ground far less warrantable, as men unbiassed will see: and that after this, we neither own, nor shall yield any willing obedience to them, they having altered and destroyed the Lord's established religion, overturned the fundamental and established laws of the kingdom, taken away altogether Christ's Church-government, and changed the civil government of this land, which was by a king and free parliament, into tyranny, where none are associate to be partakers of the government, but only those who will be found by justice to be guilty of criminals [*sic*], and where all others are excluded, even those who by the laws of the land and by birth have a right to, and a share in that government, and that only because they are not of the same guiltiness and mischievous purposes with themselves, and where also all free elections of commissioners for parliaments, and officers for government, are made void, they making those the qualifications for admission to those places which by the Word of God and the laws of the land was the cause of their exclusion before. So that none can say that we are now bound in allegiance unto them, unless they will say, we are bound in allegiance to devils whose viceregents they are, having neither authority from God (because it is by their sinfulness forfeited) nor yet judging nor ruling for God".... "We do declare, that we shall set up over ourselves, and over what God shall give us power of, government and governors according to the Word of God, and especially that word, Exodus xviii. 21: 'Moreover, thou shalt provide out of all the people able men, such as fear God, men of truth, hating covetousness; and place such over them, to be rulers of thousands, and rulers of hundreds, rulers of fifties, and rulers of tens'. That we shall no more commit the government of ourselves, and the making of laws for us, to any one single person, or lineal successor, we not being by God, as the Jews were, bound to one single family; and this kind of government by a single person being most liable to inconveniences, and aptest to degenerate into tyranny, as sad and long experience hath taught us". The paper continues under point 5 to state that the basis for the law to be set up shall be the civil and judicial, but not the ceremonial, laws of the Bible, with the exception of polygamy and divorce. This brings the paper to the end of point 5. (6) A testimony against the defections of the ministers of Scotland. "...The ministers of Christ are become the ministers of men, and bound to answer them as they will"... "If the rest had followed them, the ministry should have been extinct with themselves, and the whole work of reformation had been buried in oblivion, and not so much as the remembrance thereof kept up"... "Those ministers then not being followers of Christ, who, before Pontius Pilate gave a good confession, which was that He was a king (and no king if he had no power to order His house and subjects), and they not following Him nor his ministers, they not asserting and maintaining this His kingly power against all encroachments and usurpers of it; and besides, we being commanded if any brother walk disorderly, from such to withdraw .... we declare (which is proper for us to do) that we neither can nor will hear preaching, nor receive sacraments from any of those ministers that have accepted and voted for that liberty, nor from any who have encouraged and strengthened their hands by hearing and pleading for them, all those who have trafficked for an union with them, without their renouncing and repenting of those things, all that do not faithfully testify against them, and after do not deport themselves suitably to their testimonies, all who join not in public with their brethren who are testifying against them". (7) "Then, we do declare

and acknowledge, that a Gospel ministry is a standing
ordinance of God, appointed by Christ to continue in the
Church until the end of the world; and that none of us shall
take upon him the preaching of the Word, or administering of
the sacraments, unless called and ordained thereto by the
ministers of the Gospel". The 7th point goes on to say that in
future the calling and ordination of the ministry shall be gone
about with more prayer and fasting then formerly, and more
careful examination of the candidates. The paper then
repudiates the idea that it is schismatic or sectarian: "...for
separation, as the Scriptures and divines take it in an evil
sense, cannot be attributed to us; for if there be a separation it
must be where the change is, and that is not in us; we are not
separating from the communion of the Church, and setting up
new ordinances, and a new ministry, but cleaving to the same
ministers and following the same ordinances, when others
have slidden back to new ways, and have a new authority
superadded, which is like a new piece in the old garment".
(8) "We bind and oblige ourselves to defend ourselves and
one another in our worshipping of God, and in our natural,
civil and Divine rights and liberties, till we shall overcome, or
send them down under debate to the posterity that they may
begin where we end; and if we shall be pursued or troubled
any farther in our worshipping rights and liberties, that we
shall look on it as a declaring war, and take all the advantages
that one enemy doth of another, and seek to cause to perish
all that shall, in an hostile manner, assault us, and to
maintain, relieve, and right ourselves of those that have
wronged us, but not to trouble or injure any, but those that
have injured us, those being most lawful for us, being many
that are wronged upon such an account, and by such persons
who have nothing now over us, but power and usurped
authority, which we shall neither answer nor acknowledge, if
we can do otherwise, hoping that God shall break of that part
of the yoke, and free us of that power and tyranny that we

have cast off upon His account, and will give us judges as we had at the beginning, and councillors as we had at the first".[128]

The Queensferry Paper was never published by the Covenanters, as it was prematurely discovered and taken by the authorities. Only a few days passed, however, before the strict Covenanters published an official declaration of their principles. On the 22nd of June, 1680, Richard Cameron, accompanied by nineteen horsemen, rode to the cross in the village of Sanquhar and there read a paper which they afterwards nailed to the cross. It has been known as the Sanquhar Declaration.[129] Containing only about 850 words, it is much shorter than the Queensferry Paper. The Sanquhar Declaration lists three steps in the Reformation of the Church of Scotland: (1) From Popery. (2) From Prelacy. (3) From Erastianism. It speaks of Charles II as he "who (it is true so far as we know) is descended from the race of our kings, yet he hath so far deborded from what he ought to have been, by his perjury and usurpation in Church matters, and tyranny in matters civil, as is known by the whole land, that we have just reason to account it one of the Lord's great controversies against us, that we have not disowned him and the men of his practices, (whether inferior magistrates or any other) as enemies to our Lord and His crown, and the true Protestant and Presbyterian interest in these lands, our Lord's espoused bride and Church. Therefore, although we be for government and governors such as the Word of God and our Covenant allows, yet we for ourselves and all that will adhere to us as the representatives of the true Presbyterian Kirk and Covenanted nation of Scotland, considering the great hazard of lying under such a sin any longer, do by these presents disown Charles Stuart, that has been reigning (or rather tyrannizing as we may say) on the throne of Britain these

---

[128] Ibid., Wodrow, *op. cit.*, III, pp. 207-211.

[129] *Johnston*, op. cit., pp. 141-143.

years byegone, as having any right, title to, or interest in the said crown of Scotland for government, as forfeited several years since, by his perjury and breach of covenant both to God and His Kirk and usurpation of His crown and royal prerogatives therein, and many other breaches in matters ecclesiastic, and by his tyranny and breach of the very *leges regnandi* in matters civil. For which reason we declare, that several years since he should have been denuded of being king, ruler, or magistrate, or of having any power to act, or to be obeyed as such. As also, we being under the standard of our Lord Jesus Christ, Captain of Salvation, do declare a war with such a tyrant and usurper, and all the men of his practices, as enemies to our Lord Jesus Christ and His cause and covenants; and against all such as have strengthened him, sided with, or any wise acknowledged him in his tyranny, civil or ecclesiastic, yea, against all such as shall strengthen, side with, or any wise acknowledge any other in the like usurpation and tyranny, far more against such as would betray or deliver up our free reformed mother-kirk unto the bondage of anti-christ the Pope of Rome". The Declaration then proceeds to approve of the Testimony of Rutherglen (May 29th, 1679), and to disclaim the Glasgow declaration of June, 1679, because it takes in the King's interest, from which Scotland has been released several years. The Declaration then condemns the Duke of York, who afterwards became King James VII (II of England) as a professed Papist, and protests against his succeeding to the crown. The document closes by stating that the signers will reward those that oppose them as they have rewarded them, as the Lord gives opportunity.[130]

The Sanquhar Declaration was unsigned, but was the act of the strict Covenanters who followed Cargill and Cameron. It was the first *public* renunciation of the authority

---

[130] *Ibid.*; Wodrow, *op. cit.*, pp. 212-213.

of the House of Stuart in Scotland. Previous testimonies and sermons had set forth grievances, and condemned abuses; the Sanquhar Declaration cuts to the heart of the matter by boldly denying the right of Charles II to reign. Though the government regarded this as rebellion, still the position taken in the Declaration itself was not rebellion but revolution, not a lawless refusal to obey legitimate authority, but a formal appeal to the law of the land and to the nation as such, against tyrannical usurpation and a power which claimed to be above law.

The effect of the Queensferry Paper and the Sanquhar Declaration was to increase the troubles of the Covenanters. Cameron was killed at Ayrsmoss a few days after the publication of the Sanquhar Declaration; Cargill was captured July 11th, 1681, and soon executed. In 1681 the Parliament passed the Test Act. This was the occasion for another public protest on the part of the Cameronian Covenanters. A company of them appeared armed at the town of Lanark on January 12th, 1682, and published a declaration, which they fastened to the cross there. This document, entitled "The Act and Apologetic Declaration of the True Presbyterians of the Church of Scotland", contains 1,300 words and so is longer than the Sanquhar Declaration but much shorter than the Queensferry Paper. It declares that the Scottish Parliaments "are so prelimited by law, as that no true son of the State or Church hath liberty to sit and vote there", and asks the question, "What shall the people do in such an extremity? Should they give their reason as men, their consciences as Christians, and resign their liberties, fortunes, religion, and their all to the inexorable obstinacy, incurable wilfulness, and malice of these, who in spite of God and man (and notwithstanding of their many oaths and vows both to God and His people) are resolved to make their own will the

[131] *Johnston*, op. cit., pp. 144-147.

absolute and sovereign rule of their actions, and their strained indulgences, and the measure of the subjects' hope and happiness? Shall the end of government be lost, through weakness, wickedness, and tyranny of governors? Must the people by an implicit submission and deplorable stupidity, destroy themselves, and betray their posterity, and become objects of reproach to the present generation and pity and contempt to the future? Have they not in such an extremity good ground to make use of that natural radical power they have, to shake off that yoke, which neither we nor our forefathers were able to bear; which accordingly the Lord honoured us (in a general and, unprelimited meeting *of the estates and shires of* Scotland) to do; *a convention of unprelimited members, a convention of men who had only the glory of God and the good of the commonwealth before their eyes* ,-the like whereof the present reigning tyrant could never since his home coming pretend to? At which *convention* , he was most legally, and by general consent cast off, by the Declaration afterwards published at Sanquhar by especial warrant from the said *convention* ".

The document goes on to enumerate as grounds for the above action, "some of the many thousands of the misdemeanors of the now cast-off tyrant in his overturning of our Church and State". These included (1) The Act Rescissory, which changed the constitution of both Church and State in Scotland. (2) The King's exalting the royal prerogative above the law of the land, so as to make Scotland "a laughingstock to the neighbouring nations ...who say we have only the law of letters, instead of the letter of the law". (3) Arbitrary adjournment of parliaments. (4) Claim of supreme power over all persons and in all causes. (5) Oppressive taxation, "for keeping up a brothel, rather than a court". (6) The packed Parliament and the Test Act passed by it, "such as no Protestant (how corrupt soever) can take". The document continues, "We are only endeavouring to extricate ourselves from under a tyrannous yoke, and to reduce our Church and State to what they were in the years 1648 and 1649". It then approves the Rutherglen and Sanquhar Declarations, and proceeds to "rescind, annul, and make void" all the acts of Charles II since 1660, and particularly the acts of the Parliament which met at Edinburgh, July 28th, 1681. The closing words of the document are: "Let King Jesus Reign, and all His enemies be scattered".[132]

The government's answer soon came in the form of an act of the Privy Council which stated: "The Lords of His Majesty's Privy Council do hereby ordain any person who owns, or will not disown the late treasonable Declaration upon oath, whether they have arms or not, to be immediately put to death; this being always done in presence of two witnesses, and the person or persons having commission from the Council to that effect".[133] This order provided for military execution without any form of trial. An alternate form which provided for trial by a jury of fifteen men, to be followed by immediate execution, was used in some parts of Scotland.[134]

In 1684 the Cameronian Covenanters published another protest, entitled "The Apologetical Declaration and Admonitory Vindication against Intelligencers and Informers".[135] The document was composed by James Renwick, who was the pastor and leader of the strict Covenanters after the death of Cameron and Cargill. In it they speak of the hardships they had suffered, and of the principles which they held, and disclaimed the intention to kill

---

[132] *Ibid.*

[133] *Ibid.*, p. 147.

[134] *Ibid.*, pp. 144-147; Cf. Burton, J. H., *The History of Scotland*, III, p. 543.

[135] Johnston, *op. cit.*, p. 148; cf. Wodrow, *op. cit.*, IV, p.148.

all who differed from them, but asserted that they would regard those who persecuted them, including judges, soldiers, informants and false witnesses, as their own and God's public enemies and would deal with them accordingly.[136] The Privy Council replied to this Declaration by an ordinance issued November 22nd, 1684, by which any person who should refuse to disown the Declaration was to be instantly put to death in the presence of two witnesses.[137]

The Covenanters had openly challenged the claim of King Charles II to the throne. They had, in effect, proclaimed a revolution. For the time being they were regarded as traitors and rebels. But in a few short years, the Covenanters' rejection of tyrannical rulers became the nation's rejection, and what had been called treason and rebellion, became the deliberate act of the nation, in the Revolution of 1688.

7.   The Precise Nature of the Covenanters' Claims during the Period of Persecution.

During the twenty-eight years of persecution the Covenanters held, in brief, to the Presbyterianism of the Second Reformation, to the attainments of the Church of Scotland from 1638 to 1649. Doctrinally, they adhered to the Westminster Standards. Their special claims which resulted from the persecutions which they suffered, were set forth in the various public declarations which they issued, as well as in the sermons which were preached at the conventicles, and in the dying testimonies of the martyrs. The lengthy protests and declarations issued by the Covenanters are not nearly so complex as they appear. In general, their claims may be summarized under three heads. The special claims of the Cameronian Covenanters, in which they differed from the

[136] *Ibid.*

[137] Johnston, *op. cit.*, p. 148.

Prelatic Church of Scotland, from the indulged ministers, and from the Stuart monarchy, consisted in a practical, as distinguished from a merely theoretical, testimony for (1) The obligation upon the Church and nation of Scotland of the National Covenant and the Solemn League and Covenant; (2) The sole headship of Christ over the Church, in opposition to Erastian encroachments and tolerations; (3) Christian civil government, in opposition to absolutism.

The first claim of the Covenanters, then, was the claim that the Covenants were still binding upon the Church and nation of Scotland. To be sure, those Covenants had been repudiated by the King, and burned by the common hangman, and declared unlawful and treasonable oaths by the Parliament. But the Covenants were not common legislation that could be enacted or repealed at pleasure; they were Covenants with God, religious bonds; and the content of them being Scriptural and moral, they could not be broken or repealed without the sin of perjury. During the early years of the persecution William Guthrie, preaching on Isaiah 8 : 17-18, said, "These lands have sworn away themselves unto the Lord most solemnly, singularly, and frequently. Seven times hath Scotland been sworn away unto the Lord, in little more than the space of an hundred years. I grant, indeed, that these covenants have been broken, for which breach the Lord hath been plaguing these lands; and as there hath been no breach of covenant formerly like unto this, so I think there hath been no plague come like that which we may now expect. And yet seeing there is still a party in the land who adhere to these covenants, and have given a testimony for them, and that party is and will be accounted to the Lord for a generation, or the holy seed and substance of the land; since this is the case, God and these witnesses will not part yet if they shall abide by and adhere to these covenants".[138] Richard Cameron, years later, maintained exactly the same position. Preaching on John 5:40 he said, "They can never be satisfied. They take away your lands, but they can never take away the right of your lands. It is true, religion doth not take away the civil law; but ye know that the land was given away unto the Lord. This was included in the covenants, and they became the charters of all the lands in scotland".[139] Not only was Charles II guilty of perjury in repudiating the Covenants which he had accepted, but the nation itself was guilty of covenant breaking in receiving Charles II as king in 1660.

Cameron preaching on Hosea 13:9-10 said, "So this land has broken the covenant, and cast off the thing that is good. What is the breach of this covenant? How is it evidenced? They have 'Set up kings, but not by me: they have made princes, and I knew it not'. If this be not the case of Scotland at present I am mistaken".[140] The claim that the Covenants were still binding on the Church and nation of Scotland could only be made by the Covenanters who maintained conventicles. Such doctrine could be preached in no parish Church in Scotland, nor by any indulged minister, for the Covenants had been declared unlawful oaths, and to adhere to them was treason. And this claim was made by the Covenanters throughout the period of persecution, at the Revolution, and, indeed, down to the present day.

In the second place, the Covenanters maintained the sole headship of Christ over the Church, in opposition to Erastian encroachments and tolerations. The claim of King Charles II to supremacy in causes ecclesiastical, the

[138] Howie, John, ed., *Sermons Delivered in Times of Persecution in Scotland, by Sufferers for the Royal Prerogatives of Jesus Christ,* pp. 260-261.
[139] *Ibid.* p. 438.
[140] *Ibid.,* pp. 410-411.

Covenanters regarded as positively blasphemous. The principle of the sole headship of Christ over the Church made the Indulgence unlawful, for it proceeded from the King's Erastian supremacy over the Church. Many have condemned the Covenanters for opposing the Indulgences, but it was no controversy over trifles, for the principle of Christ's headship was involved, and the Covenanters held the high Reformed ethical principle that it is never right to make a sacrifice of principle, however slight, for the sake of practical ends or benefits. Alexander Peden, who never identified himself with the Cameronians, and yet held ground similar to theirs, said in preaching on Matthew 21:38, "And now, Sirs, I know it is neither right nor lawful for any minister or Christian in Scotland to join with others in taking houses to preach in, and to leave the fields. It were better for us all, Sirs, to go to the field in frost and snow to the knees, until we were wet to the skin, ere we bow to king, council, or one of them; for I know that the Lord will never bless the labours of one of them that have their liberty from them, whether minister or professor, but such ministers and professors shall be blasted and fruitless, and if their souls be not in hazard I am mistaken-this being the main point of our testimony, that Christ is Head of the Church and King in Zion, and this they deny on the matter. And if this be not sad and dangerous, judge ye, namely to consent to let Christ's crown go upon the head of any king in the world. And this is the sin that shall yet ruin these three lands".[141] Alexander Shields, preaching at the close of the period of persecution, said, "Although the testimony of the Church of France, and in the valleys of Piedmont, and in Hungary, be great and weighty and well worth the contending and suffering for, yet our testimony for the kingly office of Christ is more noble, and He will give it a glorious vindication when He comes to visit His people with His salvation. It is true, though the testimony for the

---

[141] *Ibid.*, p. 564.

prophetical and priestly office of Christ be noble and well worth the contending and suffering for, yet, in some respects, the kingly testimony of his kingly office is more noble and glorious, and though our testimony be so noble, yet there is not one part of it but what is opposed and contradicted not only by our enemies, but also by the ministers and professors in general. But we dare confidently affirm, and take heaven and earth to witness that we hold and maintain nothing but what is consonant and agreeable unto the word of God and the Covenanted principles of the Church of Scotland".[142] Jesus Christ is a King, and the only Head of his Church, and the liberties and powers of the Church are derived from Christ only, and not from the civil magistrate. It was because of the King's claim to supreme power in causes ecclesiastical, that so many Covenanters refused to pray for the King. Patrick Walker says that the Covenanters were willing to pray for the King in the sense of praying for the salvation of his soul, but that they would not pray for him as head of the Church of Scotland, nor would they pray for the preservation of his health and lengthening of his life as that would amount to praying that he be given increased opportunity for tyranny.[143]   Walker tells how some Covenanters were tempted to pray for the King with mental reservation: "When some of our pawky-witted primitive trucklers, in my hearing, said that they would pray for him so and so, and subscribe their allegiance to him in such and such senses; I have heard Sir George Mackenzie answer them, 'Do not cheat your own consciences, and deceive the world. Ye must pray for him, and swear allegiance to him, in the sense of the imposers; for ye that are swearers and prayers, ye have no power to put your sense upon our words' ".[144]   Just because the authorities interpreted praying for the King to

---

[142] *Ibid.*, pp. 595-596.

[143] Walker, *op. cit*, I, pp. 328-329.

[144] *Ibid.*

mean praying for him as head of the Church, the strict Covenanters refused to pray for the King, even when their lives hung in the balance of this test. The smallest yielding of ground on this point would be to compromise Christ's glorious headship over the Church of Scotland.

In the third place, the Covenanters maintained a practical testimony for Christian civil government, in opposition to absolutism. Scotland was by sacred Covenant bonds constituted a Christian and a Reformed nation. The nation deliberately, and by its own voluntary deed, in the Act of Classes, had excluded from public office men known to be opposed to the Reformation attainments of the nation. The coronation oath, sworn by Charles II at Scone in 1651, made him King upon condition of his accepting the Covenants. The Scriptures were to be the supreme standard in civil affairs as in all other affairs. Under the Scriptures, the supreme power was not the King but the nation as such, the will of the nation being expressed in free Parliaments representing the people. Over and over again the Covenanters stressed the fact that they stood for Parliamentary government as over against autocracy. They repudiated the Stuarts because Charles II had repudiated the Covenants, and because he claimed to have supreme power above the law of the land. Richard Cameron, in a sermon preached three days before his death, said that the Covenanters did not hold Chiliastic ideas, but yet they did believe in Christian civil government on earth: "Let us not be judged to be of the opinion of some men in England called the Fifth-Monarchy men, who say that, before the great day, Christ shall come in person from heaven with all the saints and martyrs and reign a thousand years on earth. But we are of the opinion that the Church shall yet be more high and glorious, as appears from the book of Revelation, and the Church shall have more power than ever she had before; and therefore we declare avowedly in opposition to all tyrannical

magistrates over Protestants, and over Presbyterians-
magistrates that are open enemies to God-we declare we will
have none such acknowledged as lawful magistrates over us.
We will have none but such as are for the advancement of
piety and the suppression of impiety and wickedness. Let all
the world say as they will, we have the word of God for
it".[145] James Renwick said that there were three reasons for
his own death: his disowning the Duke of York (James VII)
to be the lawful king of Britain; his maintenance of the
lawfulness and duty of defensive arms; and his testimony
against the sin of paying the "Cess" (a special tax levied to
support the persecution of the Covenanters); and he added
that "such a testimony was worth many lives".[146] It was
particularly because of testimony for Christian civil
government that Renwick died.

These three were the particular principles maintained
by the Covenanters in opposition to the Church and State of
their time. And these three can be reduced to a single
principle: *Ius Divinum* , divine right. The Covenanters lived
and died as witnesses for *the rights of God* . Scotland was
bound by sacred covenants to maintain the rights of God. The
rights of God included Christ's kingly office over the
Church, so the Covenanters opposed Erastianism. But the
rights of God were not limited to the ecclesiastical sphere;
they embraced every sphere and relationship of life, including
civil government. And so the Covenanters were witnesses for
the rights of God in the sphere of the civil magistracy. The
state, as well as the Church, must be Christian, Scriptural and
Reformed. It has often been stated that the Covenanters went
through twenty-eight years of persecution in a struggle for
civil and religious liberty. While there is a qualified sense in
which this is true, it is a very misleading statement. The

[145] Howie, *op. cit.*, pp. 357-358.
[146] Walker, *op. cit.*, I, p. 307.

Covenanters were not primarily interested in civil and religious liberty considered as rights of man. They never contended for civil freedom on a purely political basis, nor for religious freedom as it is understood today in the sense of universal liberty for all creeds. Their basic principle was not political, nor humanitarian, but *theocratic*. They found the rights of God revealed in Scripture, and they wished these to be practically recognized and respected in every sphere of life, including the State and the Church.

The Marquis of Argyle, when about to die on the scaffold in 1661, said, "I could die like a Roman, but choose rather to die as a Christian....God hath laid engagements upon Scotland; we are tied by Covenant to religion and reformation. It is the duty of every Christian to be loyal, yet I think the order of things is to be observed. Religion must not be the cock-boat but the ship; God must have what is His, as well as Caesar what is his".[147] Argyle died at the very beginning of the persecution, long before anyone thought of disowning Charles II, yet he sounded the keynote of the whole Covenanter movement through those twenty-eight years. Cameron, Cargill and Renwick all admitted the duty of Christians to be loyal to lawfully constituted government; but they believed in the right of revolution, and they believed that a time came when Charles II could no longer be regarded as a lawfully constituted ruler in Scotland. Just because they feared God, and were earnest in His cause, they did not hesitate to break the commandments of men.

8. Divisions among the Covenanters during the Period of Persecution.

Throughout the period of persecution the great division in Scottish Presbyterianism was naturally the division between

---

[147] Johnston, *op. cit.*, pp. 402-403.

the indulged ministers and their followers, who conformed, to a greater or less degree, to Prelacy, and the strict Covenanters who refused all compliance with Prelacy and maintained field conventicles to the bitter end. As those ministers who accepted the Indulgences were not permitted to teach the binding obligation of the Covenants, they practically forsook the ranks of the Covenanters by accepting the Indulgence; they might be Covenanters in private belief but could not be in public testimony. The very name Covenanter signifies acceptance of the Covenants as binding, and this was unlawful in the Prelatic Church in which the Indulged ministers were tolerated during their good behaviour. The division between the Indulged and the Non-indulged, therefore, was not properly a division between two classes of Covenanters, but a division between men who were silent about the binding obligation of the Covenants and men who maintained a public testimony for that obligation.

During the latter part of the persecuting period, a number of lesser divisions broke out among the Covenanters. In 1681 a Covenanter named John Gib developed fanatical tendencies and gathered about himself a little band of deluded people, four men and twenty-six women, who called themselves the Sweet Singers. Though originally Covenanters, the Gibbites repudiated not only the Covenants, but the Confession of Faith, Larger and Shorter Catechisms, Acts of the General Assembly, public declarations of the Covenanters, the metrical version of the Psalter, the division of the Bible into chapters and verses, all payment of taxes, and every minister of the Gospel in Scotland. They left their houses and went to the hills where they spent their time in fasting and chanting the penitential Psalms, while waiting for the destruction of Edinburgh. Donald Cargill visited them in the wilds, and also wrote them a letter, to persuade them of their errors, but they would not heed his warnings. They were apprehended by the authorities, and in the end most of them repented of their errors and follies.[148] The government seems to have charged the fanatical excesses of the Gibbites on the Covenanters in general, and because of this many of the martyrs from 1681 to 1688, whose testimonies are recorded in the "Cloud of Witnesses", expressly repudiated the errors of Gib.

In 1682 the followers of James Russel withdrew from the fellowship of the Covenanters, not because the latter were too strict, but because they were not strict enough to suit Russel. Patrick Walker says that Russel had had a prominent part in the killing of Archbishop Sharp, and that he was a man of a hot and fiery spirit. His reason for separation from his brethren was that they could see nothing immoral in paying toll or custom at ports and bridges, while Russel wished to make the refusal to pay such dues a condition of fellowship.[149] The Covenanters were all agreed that the Cess, a special tax levied to support the persecuting forces, was immoral and should be refused; but they were unwilling to refuse all payment of taxes or custom to the existing government, however bad it might be. The "Informatory Vindication" states that "James Russel discovered some unwarrantable excesses, pressing indifferent things as the most necessary duties, (as about naming the days of the week, and months of the year, &c.,) and otherwise imposing upon men's consciences; whereupon he and we parted; after which he branded and aspersed us with false charges, as if we had turned aside to gross defections, and palliated and plastered the corruptions of our time, consorting in this with some few, and even with some who had given little satisfying resentment of their former extravagancies with Gibb, being by them applauded and strengthened in his foresaid

---

[148] Smellie, *op. cit.*, pp. 347-348.

[149] Walker, *op. cit.*, II, p. 143, Note 5.

excesses".[150]

In 1685 the Earl of Argyle invaded Scotland with an
expedition from Holland in an attempt to redress the civil
wrongs of the land. Argyle's object appears to have been civil
and political rather than religious. The expedition was
defeated and dispersed and so ended in total failure.[151] An
attempt had been made to enlist the cooperation of the
Covenanters, which resulted in a division in the ranks of the
Covenanters. Patrick Walker writes that in April, 1685,
George Barclay and others came to the west of Scotland "in
order to engage, preach up, and prepare a people to join
Argyle, who came to Scotland about the Middle of May
thereafter, with some men and many notable arms; which
when Mr. Renwick, and the general correspondents of the
United Societies saw, his manifesto made them to demur, and
hesitate to concur in that expedition, upon these grounds and
reasons, first, because it was not concerted according to the
ancient plea of the Scottish Covenanters, in defence of our
Reformation, expressly according to our Covenants, National
and Solemn League. Secondly, because no mention was
made of these Covenants, nor of Presbyterian government, of
purpose lest the sectarian party should be irritate. Thirdly,
because it opened a door for confederacy with sectarians and
malignants. Fourthly, because of promiscuous admission into
trust (of) persons who were enemies to the cause and
accession (i.e., accessories) to the persecution, to wit,
Argyle's self, who, many times, if not always, was a
member of the bloody council, from May 1663 until 1681,
and whose vote took away the life of Mr. Donald Cargill; and
next to him, Sir John Cochran of Ochiltree, who was so
guilty of that great gush of the precious blood of Mr.

[150] *Testimony Bearing Exemplified* (Paisley, 1741,); New York, 1834, pp.
186-187.
[151] Hetherington, *op. cit.*, pp 505-506.

Cameron, and these with him at Airsmoss".[152] Barclay's attempt to enlist the help of the Covenanters failed, writes Walker, but it "kindled a fire of division amongst that people, who had been unite for five years before". "Then the simple and misled of these societies saw themselves led and left upon the ice; many of them returned with blushing to Mr. Renwick and their former societies; but never with that cordialness, love, light, life, nor zeal, as before".[153] The breach between Peden and Renwick began in 1685, and Walker states that it was caused by the activities of Barclay and others, who so influenced Peden as "to make him express himself so bitterly against Mr. Renwick, that he would set himself in opposition to him, and make his name stink above the ground".[154] It is pleasant to know that before Peden's death he was reconciled to Renwick, and asked Renwick to pray for him, after which Peden said, "Sir, I find you a faithful servant to your Master. Go on in a single dependence on the Lord, and ye shall win honestly through and cleanly off the stage".[155]

During the years of the "Killing Time" (1685-1688) the Covenanters could ill afford to be troubled by dissension among themselves. But it is impossible but that offences will come. When a man like James Russel advocated his absurd and unjustifiable views, it was absolutely necessary, both for the sake of conscience before God and for the sake of a good name among men, that he and the Covenanters should part company. When Barclay and others attempted to involve the Covenanters in a purely political project, it was absolutely necessary that they reject the temptation to join in the matter. It was to their credit that they saw the snares in their pathway

[152] Walker, *op. cit.*, I, pp. 101 ff.

[153] *Ibid.*, pp. 103 ff.

[154] *Ibid.*, p. 106.

[155] Smellie, *op. cit.*, pp. 468-469.

and kept themselves clear of such entanglements.

9.   **The Extent of the Persecution Suffered**
       by the Covenanters.

John Howie, in the conclusion to "The Scots Worthies" estimates that during the twenty-eight years of persecution in Scotland, "above 18,000 people, according to calculation, suffered death, or the utmost hardships and extremities".[156]   Of this number, he states, 1,700 were banished to America and 750 to the northern islands of Scotland. 3,600 were imprisoned, outlawed, or sentenced to be executed when apprehended. 680 were killed in skirmishes or died of their wounds. 7,000 voluntarily left Scotland for conscience' sake. 362 were executed after process of law, and 498 slaughtered without process of law. In addition to the above, "the number of those who perished through cold, hunger, and other distresses, contracted in their flight to the mountains, and who sometimes even when on the point of death were murdered by the bloody soldiers, cannot well be calculated, but will certainly make up the number above specified".[157] Alexander Smellie says that while Howie's figures may be somewhat exaggerated, yet "when everything is remembered", his figure of eighteen thousand cannot be much in excess of the grim reality".[158]

Michael Shields, in a letter written during or just after the persecuting period, enumerates some of the sufferings of the Covenanters during the reign of Charles II, speaking of "His cruelty over the bodies of Christians, in chasing and killing upon the fields, many without sentence, and bloody

---

[156] Howie, John, *The Scots Worthies*, pp. 626-627.

[157] *Ibid.*

[158] Smellie, *op. cit.*, p. 494.

butchering, hanging, heading, mangling, dismembering alive, quartering upon scaffolds, imprisoning, laying in irons, torturing by boots, thumbkins, fire-matches, cutting pieces out of the ears of others, banishing and selling as slaves old and young men and women in great numbers, oppressing many others in their estates, forfeiting, robbing, spoiling, pillaging their goods, casting them out of their habitations, interdicting any to reset them, under the pain of being treated after the same manner".[159] Cruelty was less condemned then than now; yet even if the Covenanters had been entirely wrong and the government entirely right about all the matters at issue, it would be impossible to justify the cruelties perpetrated on the Covenanters, especially the use of torture and the practice of execution without process of law. The fact is that the persecutors of the Covenanters were bloody and godless men and though they acted in the name of religion and law, they had little real regard for either.

10. The Condition of the Covenanters on the Eve of the Revolution.

During the latter part of the persecuting period the strict Covenanters, who abhorred all compliance with Prelacy and Erastianism, organized what were known as "Praying Societies" or "Society Meetings". These were private religious meetings of small groups of Covenanters, held secretly, by which they maintained their identity and refreshed their souls when field conventicles could not be held. Walter Smith, a minister who was executed in 1681, drew up a set of rules for such meetings, entitled "Rules and Directions Anent private Christian Meetings, for Prayer and Conference to mutual edification, and to the right management of the same".[160] It is interesting to note that

---

[159] MacLean, Donald, *Aspects of Scottish Church History*, p 50.

[160] Walker, *op. cit.* II, p. 94.

under rule 23, the following are listed as matters for prayer: "(1) That the old off-casten Israel for unbelief would never be forgotten, especially in these meetings, that the promised day of their ingraffing again by faith may be hastened; and that dead weight of blood removed off them, that their fathers took upon them and upon their children, that have sunk them down to hell upwards of seventeen hundred years. (2) That the Lord's written and preached word (may be sent) with power, to enlighten the poor Pagan world, living in black perishing darkness without Christ and the knowledge of his name. (3) That the damnable delusions of Mahomet, and the errors of Antichrist, Arian, Arminian, Socinian and Quakers, may be discovered; that the blind may no more lead the blind, and go to hell wholesale, living and dying so; and the many gross errors abounding among many other sectaries may come to light".[161] This shows that the followers of Cameron and Cargill were not, as they have often been represented, people interested only in bearing testimony against Prelacy, Erastianism and tyranny, whose whole religious attitude was a negative one, composed of opposition to various evils, but a people with warm evangelical faith and a zeal for the salvation of the lost, even in the heathen world. The times and the circumstances forced them to stress their testimony against particular evils, but behind all this was true Christian faith and unfeigned Christian piety.

In 1681 the Covenanter Societies were united in a "general correspondence", with a delegated meeting to be held four times yearly.[162] This form of organization was strictly non-ecclesiastical, but served as a substitute for Church organization for the Covenanters from 1681 to 1743 when the Reformed Presbytery was organized. The general correspondence was known as the United Societies.

[161] *Ibid.*

[162] *Ibid.*, p. 66; Cf. Wodrow, *op. cit.*, III, p. 357.

As the years of persecution wore away, the Covenanters became more and more convinced that the days of the Stuarts were numbered. Cameron had confidently affirmed that the Lord would remove the Stuarts from the throne, because they had usurped the kingly office of Christ.[163] A few days before his death Cameron said in a sermon, "As for that unhappy man, Charles the II who is now upon the throne of Britain, after him there shall not be a crowned king in Scotland of the name of Stewart".[164] This of course was not a prophecy but a shrewd guess; since James VII was never crowned in Scotland, Cameron was technically right, although he probably meant that Charles II would be the last of the Stuart kings. When nearly all the people of Scotland were tamely submitting to absolutist tyranny in both Church and State, Richard Cameron saw clearly that such a government could not last, that God would enable the nation to overthrow it, that the darkness would give way to the dawn, and peace and freedom be restored to the distracted land. Years before the nation as a whole the Covenanters anticipated the inevitable revolution which came in 1688. They considered themselves the legitimate representatives and continuation of the Church and State of Scotland as these had existed before the Restoration of 1660. They had appealed to the nation; they had appealed to God himself; and they awaited the outcome with grim determination not to yield or compromise, come what might. They stood for the rights of God, and endured as seeing Him who is invisible.

---

[163] Walker, *op. cit.*, I, p 227.

[164] *Ibid.*, p. 228.

CHAPTER II

THE REVOLUTION SETTLEMENT, 1688-1690.

1.   The Revolution of 1688.

In June, 1688, a son was born to King James VII, which caused alarm throughout Britain at the possibility of a line of Roman Catholic rulers. About this time seven English bishops who had been imprisoned by the King for petitioning against his arbitrary action, were tried by a court and acquitted. William of Orange saw his opportunity and sailed for England, landing on November 5th, 1688. Late in December the Scottish Privy Council by its own act dissolved; this marked the end of twenty-eight years of tyranny and persecution in Scotland. Early in 1689 a convention was held in Scotland, elected by the Protestant elements in the country,which proclaimed William and Mary King and Queen of Scotland on April 11th, 1689. The document adopted by the convention began thus: "Whereas King James VII. being a professed Papist, did assume the regal power, and acted as King, without ever taking the oath required by law, whereby the King, at his accession to the government, is obliged to swear to maintain the Protestant religion, and to rule the people according to the laudable laws, and did, by the advice of wicked and evil counsellors, invade the fundamental constitution of this kingdom, and alter it from a legal limited monarchy to an arbitrary despotic power; and, in a public proclamation, asserted an absolute power to pass, annul, and disable all the laws, particularly the laws establishing the Protestant religion, and did excercise that power to the subversion of the Protestant religion and to the violation of the laws and liberties of the kingdom...". This is followed by a list of the actions complained of, and the statement, "Therefore, the estates of the kingdom of Scotland find and declare that King James VII being a professed Papist... hath forfeited the right to the crown, and the throne is become vacant".[1] The right of revolution, the right of a nation to decide when its rulers had forfeited the right to rule, on which the Covenanters had repeatedly insisted, was now claimed and exercised, not merely by a few thousand persecuted persons, but by the Estates of Scotland, representing the whole nation, in convention assembled. Scotland was declared to be a "legal limited monarchy" and not an "arbitrary despotic power". The cause of freedom has been notably vindicated after being trampled in the dust for twenty-eight years.

In the Claim of Right prepared by the Estates, which accompanied their offer of the throne to William of Orange, Episcopacy was expressly stated to be one of the burdens under which Scotland had suffered: "Prelacy and the superiority of any officer in the Church above presbyters is, and hath been, a great and unsupportable grievance and trouble to this nation, and contrary to the inclinations of the generality of the people ever since the Reformation".[2]

2. The Legal Settlement of the Church of Scotland.

The first step in the settlement of the Church of Scotland after the Revolution was the passing by the Parliament of an "Act Rescinding the First Act of the Second Parliament of 1669". The act which was rescinded was the notorious "Act Asserting His Majesties Supremacy over all Persons and in all Causes Ecclesiastical", which was now declared to be "inconsistent with the Establishment of the

---

[1] Hetherington, W. M., *History of the Church of Scotland*, pp. 539-540.

[2] Johnston, John C., *Treasury of the Scottish Covenant*, p. 150.

Church now desired, and ought to be abrogat".[3]

On June 7th, 1690, the Parliament passed an "Act Ratifying the Confession of Faith and Settling Presbyterian Church Government".[4] Like the Claim of Right, this act called Prelacy a "great and insupportable grievance, and contrary to the inclination of the generality of the people, ever since the Reformation, they having been reformed from Popery by Presbyters". Presbyterianism was stated to be "the government of Christ's church within this nation, agreeable to the Word of God, and most conducive to the advancement of true piety and godliness, and the establishing of peace and tranquillity within this realm".[5] The act ratified the Westminster Confession of Faith, which had been ratified by Parliament in 1649. Presbyterian government was established according to the act of 1592 (The Great Charter of Presbytery), which was revived, except the part relating to patronage, which was later considered by Parliament. The act declared that "the sole power and jurisdiction within the Church" inhered in the ecclesiastical judicatories and not in the civil magistrate.[6] Presbytery was to be "the only government of Christ's Church within this Kingdom...".[7] By the terms of the act, the government of the Church of Scotland was placed in the hands of the Presbyterian ministers who had been ejected since 1661, and such ministers and elders as they should receive.[8]

It will be noted that this act of Parliament restored Presbyterian Church government as "agreeable to the Word

---

[3] *Ibid.*, p. 152.
[4] *Ibid.*, pp. 152-154.
[5] Hetherington, *op. cit.*, p. 552.
[6] Johnston, *op. cit.*, pp. 152-154.
[7] *Ibid.*
[8] Hetherington, *op. cit.*, p. 552.

Scriptural form of Church government. It is one thing to say that Presbytery is *a* form of Church government that is agreeable to the Word of God, and quite another to say that it is *the* form of Church government that is agreeable to the Word of God. King William did not believe in the divine right of any particular system of Church polity, and the Parliament in settling the government of the Church took the low ground that Church government is a matter of expediency, or a matter to be decided on the basis of the tradition and preference of the nation since the Reformation. Prelacy was rejected, but not declared to be contrary to Scripture; it was merely affirmed to have been "a great and insupportable grievance, and contrary to the inclination of the generality of the people", etc. It is plain that the character of the law was determined by policy rather than by principle. The legislation of the Revolution Settlement breathed a different spirit from that of the Second Reformation.

The Parliament of 1690, while it rescinded the act which had declared the King supreme in causes ecclesiastical, left a mass of other pernicious legislation untouched on the statute books of the nation. The Act Rescissory, which had rescinded the reforming legislation of the Second Reformation, was left untouched. The acts which condemned the National Covenant and the Solemn League and Covenant as unlawful oaths, and the act which called the General Assembly of 1638 an unlawful and seditious Assembly, as well as other similar laws, were left untouched.[9] Patronage was indeed abolished, but in its place a system was instituted by which the heritors and elders of a parish were given the right to nominate a minister when the parish was vacant, and the people themselves were to be permitted to accept or reject the candidate.[10]

---

[9] Johnston, *op. cit.*, pp. 150-152.

[10] Smellie, Alexander, *Men of the Covenant*, p. 505.

Of the ministers who had been ejected since 1661, only sixty were still living in 1690,[11] and by these the General Assembly was constituted after an interval of thirty-seven years since the last Assembly had been dispersed by Cromwell's soldiers. The ministers who had been entrusted by Parliament with the government of the Church held a preliminary meeting to make arrangements for the General Assembly, which set up presbyteries and instructed these concerning the election of commissioners to the General Assembly.[12] When the Assembly met on October 16th, 1690, one hundred and sixteen ministers and forty-seven ruling elders were present as commissioners from the presbyteries.[13]

At this period there were some nine hundred parishes in Scotland, all of which had been occupied by men who had conformed to Episcopacy. Large numbers of these were soon received into the Revolution Church without any real evidence of a hearty acceptance of the Presbyterian polity. In 1693 the Parliament passed an act which required all ministers of the Church of Scotland to subscribe the Confession of Faith, and to approve of Presbyterian government, not as the only Scriptural polity, but as the only government of the Church of Scotland.[14] This permitted large numbers of the former "curates", men who had supported a government which had persecuted the Church and slaughtered the saints of God, to be received into the ministry of the Revolution Church while still believing that Prelacy is a Scriptural form of Church government. These former Episcopalians formed what later became known as the

---

[11] *Ibid.*, p. 504.

[12] Grub, George, *An Ecclesiastical History of Scotland from the Introduction of Christianity to the Present Time*, III, pp. 322-323.

[13] Smellie, *op. cit.*, p. 508.

[14] Johnston, *op. cit.*, p. 156.

"Moderate" party in the Church of Scotland, that party which nearly extinguished evangelical religion and orthodoxy in the Church in later years.[15]

Presbyterianism had indeed been restored, but the wrongs of the persecuting period had by no means all been undone. The Covenants were still trampled in the dust. The divine right of Presbytery was not asserted. Prelacy was not condemned as unscriptural. The whole fabric of the Revolution Settlement was too much the work of the civil magistrate. Large numbers of the "curates" were admitted without adequate examination and safeguards. The Church of the Revolution Settlement had a pliable, tolerant spirit very different from the strict adherence to principle which characterized the Church of the Second Reformation. The nation as a whole was weary of strife and difficulties, and human nature being what it is, it is not surprising that the Parliament and General Assembly followed a broad *via media* between opposite views in reconstructing the Church of Scotland.

3.   Attitude of the Covenanters to the Revolution Settlement.

Between the Revolution and the first meeting of the General Assembly, the Cameronian Covenanters solemnly renewed the Covenants at a place called Borland Hill, near Lesmahagow, on March 3rd, 1689.[16] The service was attended by a large number of members of the United Societies, and was conducted by the three Cameronian ministers, Shields, Linning and Boyd. Shields publicly confessed his sin in having formerly complied with various

---

[15] *Ibid.*, pp. 150-152.

[16] *Ibid.*, p.163.

evils, to the satisfaction of those present.[17]   Thus at this critical juncture in the history of the Scottish Church and nation did those who still adhered to the Covenants proclaim their faith and purpose to the world.

After the Revolution Settlement, the United Societies petitioned the General Assembly to redress their grievances. Patrick Walker was one of the brethren appointed to present the matter to the Assembly. He writes, "We were long put off, and with great difficulty got them laid before them, many of them about the helm looking upon us with a frowning countenance; and when we saw many of our bitter tongued persecutors sitting there as elders, and had so little regard to our grievances, and esteem of us, that they thought it not worth their while to give us any answer; these and other things made us come out with our hearts filled with sorrow".[18]   It is clear from this that the General Assembly was not minded to look carefully into the matters urged by the Covenanters.

The Cameronian ministers, Shields, Boyd and Linning presented two papers to the General Assembly, a longer and a shorter one, in which they urged the consideration of the points for which Covenanters had contended. At the same time they applied for admission to the ministry of the Revolution Church, and promised to be subject to the judicatories of the Church and to oppose schism and defection. Their application came before the Assembly on October 25th, 1690, by a report from the Committee on Overtures.[19]   The Committee recommended that the shorter of the two papers be read to the Assembly, but stated that the reading of the longer one would be "inconvenient, in regard

---

[17] *Ibid.*

[18] Walker, Patrick, *Six Saints of the Covenant*, I, p. 259.

[19] *Ibid.* II. p.173.

that though there be several good things in it, yet the same doth also contain several peremptory and gross mistakes, unseasonable and impracticable proposals, and uncharitable and injurious reflections, tending rather to kindle contentions than to compose divisions".[20] Shields, Boyd and Linning then appeared before the Assembly and acknowledged their shorter paper, after which the Assembly, without a dissenting vote, adopted the report of the Committee.[21]

Alexander Shields also presented a petition to the Parliament, in the name of "the persecuted people of the west and southern shires," setting forth the claims, and requests of the Covenanters. This paper was rejected by a committee of Parliament and never reached the floor of Parliament itself.[22]

In spite of the unsatisfactory way in which the General Assembly had dealt with their papers, the three Covenanter ministers, Shields, Linning and Boyd, entered the Revolution Church. Patrick Walker says that in later years Shields regretted that he had not taken a more positive attitude when the matters were before the General Assembly: "Mr. Shields much lamented his silence before the Assembly, and coming so far short of his former resolutions, 'that if he ever saw such an occasion, he should not be tonguetacked': Masters Linning and Boyd had two much influence with him, being in haste for kirks, stipends and wives".[23] Walker reports a conversation with Shields, in which the latter defended his entrance into the Revolution Church on the ground that there were many good men in it: "And Mr. Shields said to me, in our last parting at Edinburgh before he went abroad, 'Altho' ye have many naughty ministers in this

---

[20] *Ibid.*

[21] *Ibid.*

[22] *Ibid.*, II, p. 174.

[23] *Ibid.*, I, p. 260.

Church, yet ye have some worthy men; cleave to the best, for it is not only dreadfully dangerous to separate from all, but utterly unwarrantable and cannot be defended; wait on, for I am perswaded there is somewhat coming upon this Church that will pull you out of doubts of withdrawing from the most part' ".[24] This amounted to deciding the question of union or separation on the basis of the character of the ministers in the Church, rather than on the basis of the official creedal and legal position of the Church.

Alexander Smellie writes in "Men of the Covenant" that three of the Cameronian ministers, "but only three", united with the Established Church after the Revolution, while "the inflexible majority, true to themselves and hating all paltering and accommodation, refused to countenance arrangements which were not the highest but merely the next to the highest. Thankful as their inexorable souls were when 'the new sun rose bringing the new year', they recognized with sadness that even this nobler and joyfuller epoch was not that *acceptable year of the Lord* for which they had prayed and bled".[25] This statement seems to imply that at the time of the Revolution Settlement, the Cameronians had a large number of ministers, of whom only three entered the Revolution Church, while the majority remained separate. The fact that at the time of the Revolution Settlement the Cameronians had only three official preachers, namely Shields, Linning and Boyd, and that all of these entered the Established Church, which left the Covenanters without a minister until the accession of John Macmillan sixteen years later. Apart from this, Smellie's statement of the matter is very weak. The Covenanters regarded the Revolution Settlement, not merely as something "next to the highest", but as something positively sinful, as will be shown below. Their

---

[24] *Ibid.*, I, p. 292.

[25] Smellie, *op. cit.*, p. 506.

three ministers forsook them and entered the Established Church, and part of the lay membership, of whom Patrick Walker was one, did the same, but the United Societies as such remained aloof and continued their non-ecclesiastical form of organization until 1743 when the Reformed Presbytery was organized as the spiritual continuation of the General Assembly dispersed by Cromwell's soldiers in 1653.

4. The Covenanters' Grounds for Dissent from the Revolution Settlement.

The Testimony which the Reformed Presbytery adopted at Ploughlandhead in 1761 sets forth in considerable detail the grounds of the United Societies for dissent from the Revolution Settlement.[26] This document gives not only the grounds for dissent from the Established Church of the Revolution Settlement, but also for dissent from the constitution of the State which resulted from the Revolution. It begins with reasons for dissent from the civil constitution, objecting first to King William and Queen Mary, because they were foreigners, and had been educated in an Erastian Church, which is stated to be contrary to Deuteronomy 17:15, "Thou shalt in any wise set him king over thee, whom the Lord thy God shall choose: one from among thy brethren shalt thou set king over thee: thou mayest not set a stranger over thee, which is not thy brother". To this it is added that William and Mary lacked not only Scriptural, but also covenant qualifications, "namely, known integrity, approven fidelity, constant affection, and zeal to the cause and true church of GOD; and therefore could not in a consistency with the covenanted constitution, and fundamental laws of the crown, be set up as king and queen of these covenanted lands".[27] The next objection is to the character of the

---

[26] *Act, Declaration, and Testimony*, (Ploughlandhead, Scotland, 1761); Philadelphia, 1876, pp. 54-72.

[27] *Ibid.*, p. 55.

membership of the Committee of Estates and first Parliament of the Revolution, namely that these were made up of persons who had persecuted the Church, and who had made no confession of having done wrong in this, and were therefore not qualified to represent the kingdom. After this, objection is made to the character of the constitution itself: "Although the declaration of the meeting of estates in this kingdom, containing their claim of right, comprehended much more of their civil liberties, and formal rights of government, than was enjoyed under the former monstrous tyranny, yet by no means sufficiently provided for the legal establishment of our former happy reformed constitution, which necessarily obliged the civil rulers to employ their power to maintain and defend, not only the doctrine, but also the presbyterian worship, discipline and government, as the only and unalterable form instituted by Christ in his house". [28] Prelacy was rejected, but not declared to be unscriptural; Presbytery was adopted, but not declared to be of divine right; the Confession of Faith was adopted by the Parliament, but not declared to be of Scriptural authority. [29]

This is followed by objections to the ecclesiastical constitution, and first to the ministers who first composed it: "That the members composing the same were no less, if not much more exceptionable, than those of whom the state consisted; the whole of them one way or another being justly chargeable with unfaithfulness to CHRIST, and his covenanted cause, by sinful and scandalous compliance with the public defections of the former times, or actively countenancing the malignant apostasy of the lands, which will appear evident, by considering that the Revolution Church consisted of such office-bearers, as had, in contradiction to their most solemn covenant engagements,

---

[28] *Ibid.*, pp. 56-57.

[29] *Ibid.*, p. 57.

fallen in with, and approven of the public resolutions".[30] The office-bearers of the Revolution Church are also objected to because they had all submitted to the Indulgences at least to the last one of James VII which is called a "blasphemous unbounded toleration, which that popish tyrant, the duke of *York*...granted, with a special view to reintroduce abjured popery; and therefore while it extended its protection to every heresy, did exclude the pure preaching of the gospel in the fields; which toleration...was joyfully embraced by all the presbyterian ministers in Scotland, the honored Mr. Renwick only excepted, who faithfully protested against the same".[31] A further objection to the officers of the Revolution Church is that they were polluted by wicked oaths, or by "approving the warrantableness of giving security to the bloody council, not to exercise their ministry, but according to their pleasure".[32]

Next come objections to the Revolution Church itself, because Erastian in character and therefore inconsistent with the constitution of the Church in 1648, as evidence of which the statute of 1592 is cited, which provided for the time and place of meetings of the General Assembly to be appointed by the King's commissioner; and this is stated by the Testimony to be "a manifest invasion and traitorous attack...upon the headship and supremacy of Christ, as a Son in, and over his own house. He who is God's anointed King in Zion, and sits on the throne of his holiness, is hereby robbed of his crown rights; the intrinsic power, the spiritual liberty and freedom, granted by Christ to his church, is encroached upon. It is a received opinion among all true Presbyterians, that the church hath an intrinsic power to meet in the the courts of Christ's house, from the lowest to the highest, by virtue of the power committed to her by the Lord Jesus Christ, without

---

[30] *Ibid.*, pp. 57-58.

[31] *Ibid.*, p. 58.

[32] *Ibid.*, p. 59.

dependence on the civil power".[33]   It is stated that the Revolution Church is Erastian in the same sense that the Prelatic Church was before the Revolution: "As the Episcopalians owned the king, in the exercise of his Erastian supremacy over them, so the Revolution Church, instead of opposing, did take up her standing under the covert of that antichristian supremacy, and has never since declined the exercise thereof. And, as the civil power prescribed limits unto, and at pleasure altered, the prelatic church, so this church has accepted of a formula, prescribed by the civil power, requiring that all ordinances within the same be performed by the ministers thereof, as they were then allowed them, or should thereafter be declared by their authority, as *act* 23d, *sess*. 4th, *parl*. 1st, 1693, expressly bears".[34]

The Testimony further objects to the Revolution Church because its constitution was modelled on the act of 1592 (Great Charter of Presbytery) and not on the constitution of the Church of the Second Reformation as, it was in 1648, and states that "therefore, this revolution constitution amounts to a shameful disregarding- yea, disclaiming and burying- much (if not all) of the reformation attained to in that memorable period,and is a virtual homologation and allowance of the iniquitous laws at the restoration, *anno* 1661, condemning our glorious reformation and sacred covenant as rebellion; and as such an aggravated step of defection and apostasy, as to clearly discovers this church to be fixed upon a different footing and to be called by another name, than the genuine offspring of the true covenanted church of Christ in *Scotland* ".[35]

Following the above come special items of objection

---

[33] *Ibid.*, p 60.

[34] *Ibid.*, p. 61.

[35] *Ibid.*, p. 62.

to the settlement of religion in Scotland at the time of the Revolution. The first is that Prelacy was continued in England and Ireland, contrary to the Solemn League and Covenant.[36] Second, the covenanted Reformation in Scotland as it existed from 1638 to 1650, was not restored, but left "buried under the infamous act recissory, which did, at one blow, rescind and annul the whole of the reformation, and authority establishing the same, by making a retrograde motion, as far back as 1592, without ever coming one step forward since that time, and herein acted most contrary to the practice of our honored reformers, who always used to begin where former reformations stopped, and after having removed what obstructed the work of reformation, went forward in building and beautifying the house of the Lord".[37] Third, because the settlement was Erastian in method, in that the lead was taken by the State, not by the Church: "Instead of setting the church foremost in the work of the Lord, and the State coming after, and ratifying by their civil sanction what the church had done; the Revolution parliament inverted this beautiful order, both in abolishing prelacy, settling presbytery, and ratifying the Confession of Faith, as the standard of doctrine to this church".[38] The Testimony affirms that the method used in the Revolution Settlement is condemned by the very language of the Confession of Faith itself, in chapter xxiii section 3, which says that "The civil magistrate may not assume to himself the administration of the word or the keys"; and also that the method used is condemned "by the beautiful practice of our reformers, betwixt 1638 and 1649, who observed the scriptural order, the church always going foremost, in all the several pieces of reformation attained to, and then the state coming after, by exerting their authority, in ratification and defense of the

---

[36] *Ibid.*, pp. 62-63.

[37] *Ibid.*, p. 63.

[38] *Ibid.*, p. 65.

church's acts and deeds, in behalf of reformation".[39] At this
point the objection to the Act of 1592 is repeated, and it is
stated that as the Revolution Settlement was based on the Act
of 1592, it cannot "be freed of the charge of Erastianism",
because "that act 1592 contains an invasion upon the
headship of Christ, and intrinsic power of the church, and
ascribes an Erastian power to the civil magistrate over the
church, making it unlawful for the church to convocate her
superior judicatories, but in dependence upon the king for his
license and authority".[40] Finally, the Revolution settlement is
objected to, because founded on policy, not on principle;
King William instructed the Parliament in 1690, "You are to
pass an act establishing that church government which is
most agreeable to the inclinations of the people", and the
Parliament passed an act, "Settling Presbyterian church
government in the same form, and on the same footing", i.e.,
without declaring it to be of divine right.[41]

The Ploughlandhead Testimony sums up its reasons
for dissent from the Revolution Settlement as follows:
"Hence we have the idolatrous institutions of prelacy
established in the one nation, and Erastianism, under the
specious pretext of presbytery, on the other; and both under
an exotic head of ecclesiastical government". "From what is
said above, respecting the Revolution constitution, and
settlement of religion in the nations, it will appear, that the
same are opposite to the word of God, and covenanted
institutions of both church and state, and to the reforming
laws, between 1638 and 1650, ratifying and securing the
doctrine, worship, discipline, and government of the church,
and all divine ordinances, sacred and civil, according to
scriptural revelation; and therefore cannot be acknowledged

---

[39] *Ibid.*, p. 67.

[40] *Ibid.*

[41] *Ibid.*, p. 69.

as lawful, by any that make the law of God their rule, and desire to go out by the footsteps of the flock of Christ". [42]

From the foregoing it will be seen (1) that the Covenanters objected not only to the Revolution Church but to the constitution of the Revolution State; (2) that they objected to the Revolution Settlement of religion as being retrogressive rather than progressive, since it stood upon the ground of 1592 not of 1648; (3) that they maintained the continuing validity, and binding obligation on the Church and nation, of the National Covenant and Solemn League and Covenant, and objected to the Revolution Settlement because these were ignored, or even violated; (4) that they objected to the Erastianism, in both method and character, of the Revolution Settlement, as contrary to Scripture and the past attainments of the Church of Scotland; (5) that they objected to the *persons* placed in authority in both Church and State, as having been implicated in the gross evils of the former reigns, and having done nothing to clear themselves or show themselves worthy of the confidence of the Church and nation; (6) that they objected to the persons of the King and Queen themselves, because they were foreigners, former members of an Erastian Church, and not bound by the Scottish Covenants.

While the claims and protests of the Covenanters were practically, if not entirely, disregarded at the time of the Revolution Settlement, the subsequent history of the Church of Scotland has demonstrated that they were right in their assertion that the Revolution Church was perverted by Erastianism. The whole history of the patronage controversy, and of the Secession and Relief movements, shows that the Revolution Church was in bondage to the civil magistrate. The Cameronians, who were the only people in Scotland

---

[42] *Ibid.*, pp. 71-72.

publicly maintaining the Covenants, remained out of the Revolution Church. The Seceders soon came out, and then they too maintained the continuing obligation of the Covenants. The Secession justified the Covenanters in their original refusal to incorporate with the Revolution Church; if Erastianism in practice justified the Secession, then Erastianism in principle, to which the Covenanters objected in 1690, justified the refusal to incorporate with the Church at that time. The principal difference between the Covenanters in 1690 and the Seceders in 1733 was that the Seceders objected to the Erastian constitution and practices of the Church, while the Covenanters objected not only to these but to the constitution of the State which resulted in an Erastian Church.

It should be stated at this point that the Covenanters or Cameronians, who later became the Reformed Presbyterian Church, cannot be regarded as having seceded, withdrawn or separated from the Church of Scotland, because *they never were in ecclesiastical union with the Revolution Church* ; they remained separate from that body, but at no time became separate from it. For twenty-eight years the Church of Scotland as by law established had been an Episcopal Church; before that, it had been the Presbyterian Church of the Second Reformation. That body of people which became the Reformed Presbytery in 1743 traced an unbroken line, not indeed of ecclesiastical organization, but of dissent and separate worship, first from the Episcopal Church, and later from the Revolution Church, which extended from the Church of the Second Reformation to the organization of the Reformed Presbytery. When the Reformed Presbytery was organized in 1743, therefore, it was not a schismatic or sectarian organization; no rending of the body of Christ took place, but only the attainment of ecclesiastical organization of those who had never been in ecclesiastical union with the Church of the Revolution Settlement. There are two ecclesiastical bodies in Scotland today which are Presbyterian Churches and which have never separated from any other Presbyterian body. One is the Church of Scotland, and the other is the Reformed Presbyterian Church. Neither can trace a continuous ecclesiastical organization back to the Church of the Second Reformation, for the Church of Scotland was by law Episcopalian from the Restoration to the Revolution. The claim of either, then, to represent the Church of the Second Reformation period, must rest not upon continuity of organization but if anything upon identity of principles. Upon this the Reformed Presbytery, in the Ploughlandhead Testimony of 1761, rested its case, and that Testimony is a detailed argument which purports to demonstrate that the Reformed Presbytery did, and the Church of the Revolution Settlement did not, maintain the principles of the Church of the Second Reformation. Since there was an obvious difference between the constitution of the Church of Scotland in 1592 and that in 1648, and since the Act Rescissory was left on the statute book at the Revolution, and the Revolution Church was founded on the revived statute of 1592 and not on the laws existing in 1648, the contention of the Covenanters that the Church of the Revolution Settlement was not the legitimate continuation of the Church of the Second Reformation must be allowed as valid. Whether the Church of the Revolution Settlement was better, wiser, or more expedient than the Church of the Second Reformation may be regarded as debatable; but concerning the question of the identity or difference of the principles on which the two were founded, there can be no debate. The Church of the Revolution Settlement claimed to be the Church of Scotland as by law established, but it did not claim to be founded on the principles and laws which were the basis of the Church of the Second Reformation.

Something should be said here about what aims of the

Covenanters were realised at the time of the Revolution. It
has often been stated as an obvious thing that the Covenanters
were struggling through the period of persecution for civil
and religious liberty. This is true in a sense, but not in the
modern sense in which the terms civil and religious liberty are
commonly used today. They strove primarily for the *rights of
God* in both Church and State, and for the rights of men
only as they regarded these as in harmony with the rights of
God. They always approved of the legislation restricting the
civil rights of Roman Catholics; and the National Covenant
which was the very textbook of the Covenanting movement
approved of the acts of Parliament which "ordain all Papists
and Priests to be punished with manifold civil and
ecclesiastical pains, as adversaries to God's true religion,
preached, and by law established, within this realm".[43] The
Ploughlandhead Testimony, 1761, testifies against Oliver
Cromwell that he "framed a hellish and almost unbounded
toleration in Scotland, of heretical and sectarian errors",[44] and
against the Act of 1712 which granted toleration and legal
protection to Episcopalianism in Scotland, as "a sinful and
almost boundless toleration",[45] which would enable "all sects
and heretics (popish recusants and anti-trinitarians some way
excepted, who yet are numerous in the nation), to make
whatever attacks they please upon the kingdom and interest of
our glorious Redeemer, in order to the advancement of their
own and the devil's, and all with impunity".[46] The Reformed
Presbytery likewise objected to the taking away of the civil
pains of excommunication, in 1712, and the provision that
none could be compelled by the civil magistrate to appear
before ecclesiastical judicatories.[47] To affirm, then, that the

---

[43] National Covenant (1638), Second Part (List of Acts of Parliament, etc.).

[44] *Act, Declaration and Testimony*, p. 22.

[45] *Ibid.*, p. 89.

[46] *Ibid.*

[47] *Ibid.*

Scottish Covenanters, during the persecuting and post-revolution periods, believed in civil and religious liberty, as these terms are understood today, is an unhistorical anachronism. They claimed liberty for themselves, but protested when it was extended to Episcopalians, because they maintained that themselves were right, and the Episcopalians were wrong, and the civil magistrate should support and protect what was right, and not what was wrong. This is very different from the modern doctrine that all religions, so long as they are peaceable and law-abiding, and do nothing which menaces the good order of civil society, are entitled to the protection of the civil magistrate. The Covenanters held no such doctrine; the whole idea of the distinction between civil right and moral right does not seem to have occurred to them.

But civil freedom in the sense of freedom from absolutist or arbitrary government, and religious freedom in the sense of freedom to practice and propagate the religion revealed in the Word of God, were undoubtedly among the things for which the Covenanters contended throughout the period of persecution, and both of these they attained in the Revolution. Arbitrary government was at an end; thenceforth the government was to be not an absolute, but a limited, constitutional monarchy. Religious persecution, so far as the Covenanters were concerned, was at an end; henceforth no man troubled them. They could even publicly disown the constitution of the Revolution State as immoral, without the slightest danger. The battle for liberty had been won.

Another principle for which the Covenanters had contended, which was vindicated in the Revolution, was the principle that a nation has the right to judge when a ruler has forfeited his title to the throne. This right of revolution was boldly asserted by the Covenanters years before it was exercised by the nation as such, and to the followers of Cameron, Cargill and Renwick belongs the honor of having contended for this priceless principle through the time when to do so often meant resisting unto blood. When Charles I was executed by the English Commonwealth, the Scottish Covenanters of that period disapproved and condemned the act; they were still filled with an almost blind loyalty to the Stuarts. When Cameron and his followers posted the Sanquhar Declaration, and openly renounced the authority of Charles II, it was an act of the greatest daring, for which many of them paid with their lives within a few weeks. Of all the population of Scotland, only a few thousand held that the deed was righteous. Cameron, Cargill and Renwick all lost their lives because they held the principles set forth in the Sanquhar Declaration. Yet they were vindicated by the Revolution, when the nation dethroned James VII and gave the crown to William of Orange in his stead. Henceforth no king in Britain could claim to hold his crown directly from God apart from the consent of the nation.

But apart from the things which have been mentioned, the Covenanters gained at the Revolution little or nothing of the things for which they had contended. Their whole testimony against Erastianism, in favor of the continuing obligation of the Covenants, and in favor of their conception of Christian civil government, was not realised, and became their ground of dissent from the Revolution Church and State.

CHAPTER III

THE
REFORMED PRESBYTERIANS SINCE THE
REVOLUTION

**1.   The Accession of John Macmillan to
        the Covenanting Societies.**

The United Societies had been organized in 1681, and it was not until 1743 that an ecclesiastical form of organization was attained. From the Revolution Settlement in 1690 to the accession of Macmillan in 1706, the Societies were without an ordained pastor, and since it was against their principles to hear the preaching of, or receive the sacraments from, the ministers of the Revolution Church, there was a period of sixteen years during which they were deprived of the ministry of the Word and the sacraments. The only exception to this was that the Rev. David Houston, Covenanting minister in Ireland, ministered ordinances to Covenanters from Scotland who resorted to him.[1] Houston died in 1696, leaving the Covenanters of Britain and Ireland entirely without a ministry. They continued to meet for worship in "Society Meetings", the services usually being led by the elders.

John Macmillan was born in 1659 of parents who attended the services of the Prelatic Church. He studied at the University of Edinburgh, and later became associated with the United Societies. After a time he left them, however, and

[1] *Testimony of the Reformed Presbyterian Church of Ireland*, Part II (Historical), p. 98.

in 1700 he was licensed in the Revolution Church,[2] and later ordained, becoming pastor of the parish of Balmaghie.

In 1702 the Synod of Galloway directed the ministers under its jurisdiction to explain the National Covenant to their congregations. Macmillan, who had a zeal for the Covenants, took counsel with the Balmaghie Session, and with their approval, added to the National Covenant the Solemn League and Covenant, and expounded both.[3]

There was some controversy about the oath of allegiance imposed on the accession of Queen Anne. The presbytery to which Macmillan belonged decided to leave the taking or not taking of the oath an open question, but this did not satisfy Macmillan, who filed a protest with the presbytery, complaining not only about their attitude toward the oath, but about the whole constitution of the Church of the Revolution Settlement. The presbytery was unmoved by Macmillan's complaint, and attempted, somewhat lamely, to refute his arguments.[4] Macmillan became so disgusted that he decided to stop attending presbytery meetings. The presbytery dealt with him and he promised to resume attendance, but later retracted this promise. The presbytery was about to try him when Macmillan declined its authority and appealed to the "first free and lawfully constituted General Assembly of the Church of Scotland".[5] The next day, in his absence, Macmillan was deposed from the office of the ministry. He continued to occupy his pulpit, was summoned to appear before the General Assembly, failed to appear, and finally in June, 1704, met with the Assembly's

[2] Hutchison, Matthew, *The Reformed Presbyterian Church in Scotland. Its Origin and History, 1680-1876*, p. 140.

[3] *Ibid.*, p. 141.

[4] *Ibid.*, p. 142.

[5] *Ibid.*, p. 143.

Commission. In July he signed a paper acknowledging his great sin in leaving off attending presbytery meetings and in declining the authority of the Presbytery of Kirkcudbright.[6] After this Macmillan appealed to the presbytery to revoke the sentence of deposition against him, but this was not done. He then retracted the promises he had made to the Assembly's Commission, of obedience to ecclesiastical authority, and renewed his appeal to the "first free and lawfully constituted General Assembly of the Church of Scotland". In 1705 he addressed an appeal to the General Assembly of the Revolution Church.[7] Because he continued to occupy his pulpit in spite of the sentence of deposition against him, he was summoned to appear before the Privy Council at Edinburgh, but failed to do so. Three years after his deposition, Macmillan was still preaching in his parish Church and had possession of the manse and glebe.[8]

While these negotiations were going on, Macmillan was also carrying on negotiations in another direction, namely with the United Societies, of which he had once been a member but whose fellowship he had forsaken to seek licensure and ordination in the Established Church. The Societies approved of Macmillan's zeal for the Covenants and of his disapprobation of the evils of the Revolution Settlement. They needed a minister badly, having been without ordinances for years. But before they would receive Macmillan they required him to confess his sin in leaving them and conforming to the Revolution Church. This procedure was not unique in Macmillan's case; the Societies followed it in the case of all persons who had conformed to the Revolution Church. On August 14th, 1706, Macmillan signed the required confession, as follows: "I, Mr John

---

[6] *Ibid.*, p. 145.
[7] *Ibid.*, p. 146.
[8] *Ibid.*, pp. 147-148.

M'Millan, minister at Balmaghie, having displeased the Godly Remnant and greatly offended them before I entered the ministry, and that in my leaving them when then joined with them, and also since, in tampering with the ministers after I had declined them, which I desire to lament, do oblige myself, for Truth's vindication, and the Godly Remnant's satisfaction, to stand to the determination of any faithful, lawfully constituted Church Judicatory of Christ within this land when it shall happen to be, which both they and I can own, submit to and concur with according to the comely order of the Church in her best times, in whatever has been sinful or offensive in my walk, way or carriage, ever since I left them to this very day. As witness my hand, at Crawfordjohn, this 14th day of August, 1706. Sic subscr. J. M'Millan".[9]

The next day Macmillan signed an additional paper approving of the position taken by the United Societies: "I, John M'Millan, minister at Balmaghie, heartily approve of, assent to and comply with all the Testimonies that have been carried on with respect to the Covenanted Reformation, and that in the by-past and present times by the honest godly and faithful Remnant against both Church and State, as they were and are agreeable to the Word of God and the Covenanted work of Reformation, as witness my hand, at Crawfordjohn, this 15th day of August, 1706. J. M'Millan".[10]

At this time the United Societies were about twenty in number, with a total membership of some seven thousand.[11] Having satisfied themselves as to the soundness of

---

[9] *Ibid.*, pp. 150-151.

[10] *Ibid.*, p. 151.

[11] *Summary of the Testimony of the Reformed Presbyterian Church of Scotland*, p. 35.

Macmillan, they extended to him a call to be their pastor.[12] Macmillan accepted the call and became pastor-at-large to the seven thousand members of the twenty or more Societies, which were not divided into congregations. In addition to this Macmillan continued to live in the manse at Balmaghie and to occupy the pulpit when at home. He divided his time between preaching in the parish Church there and itinerating among the scattered Covenanter Societies.

Although it took Macmillan a long time to make up his mind to separate entirely from the Revolution Church and identify himself exclusively with the Covenanters, the evidence indicates that when he finally did so, he became a strict Cameronian. Patrick Walker, who seems to have cherished a hearty dislike for Macmillan and his followers, reports an illustrative incident: "Notwithstanding I can instruct place and persons, where Mr. M'Millan refused baptism to an honest man's child, asking no other question, but, 'If he paid the cess'. He said, 'It was not required of him'. Mr. M'Millan said, 'If it were, would he pay it?' He answered, 'He would, for he did not look upon the paying of it now, as in the time of persecution'. He said, 'He would administer Church privileges to none who were of that judgment' ". [13]

Walker, who had been a member of the United Societies but left them after the Revolution, also asserts that only a minority of the United Societies adhered to Macmillan and his party: "All know that it was the fewest number of the United Societies, that was led off with Robert Hamilton to the disowning of King William as King of Britain and his Government; the greater part reckoned it their duty to take a

---

[12] *Testimony of the Reformed Presbyterian Church of Ireland*, Part II (Historical), p. 107.

[13] Walker, Patrick, *Six Saints of the Covenant*, I, p. 144.

legal unite way of witnessing, by humble pleadings, representations, and protestations, pleading for and with their mother to put away her whoredoms".[14]   The Robert Hamilton referred to was one of the Covenanters who had participated in publication of the Rutherglen Testimony in 1679.

After the Revolution part of the members of the United Societies wished to renew the Covenants in such a way as to include a pledge of allegiance to William of Orange. Hamilton opposed this plan so vigorously that it was defeated.[15] When the United Societies called M'Millan to be their pastor in 1706, the action was taken by the Societies as a body; therefore Walker's statement cited above must mean that the majority of those who before the Revolution adhered to the United Societies, left the Societies after the Revolution, earlier or later, and joined the Revolution Church, so that only a minority of the pre-Revolution membership of the Societies retained membership in them and adhered to Hamilton and Macmillan.

In 1712 the Societies renewed the National Covenant and the Solemn League and Covenant at Auchensaugh. The occasion for this act was a double one. They objected to the treaty of union between Scotland and England (1707) and to the Act of Toleration (1712) which gave legal protection to Episcopalian worship in Scotland. The renovation of the Covenants took several days. The members swore to the Solemn League and Covenant with uplifted hands, article by article.[16]

---

[14] *Ibid.*, p. 147.

[15] *Testimony of the Reformed Presbyterian Church of Ireland*, Part II (Historical), p. 106.

[16] Johnston, John C., *Treasury of the Scottish Covenant*, p. 163.

Not long after Macmillan's accession to the United Societies, a licentiate named John Macneill was received by them. Macneill had been licensed during the period of persecution, by the Presbytery of Penpont, 1669. He held the same views as Macmillan and joined him in his appeal to the General Assembly in 1708. The United Societies refused to ordain him as they had only one minister and no presbytery. Macneill continued as a licentiate and preached for the Covenanters until his death in 1732. He was never ordained, and when he died he had been a licentiate for sixty-three years.[17]

2.   The Organization of the Reformed Presbytery, 1743.

The Covenanters' lack of a presbytery caused them to lose another candidate for the ministry, Andrew Clarkson, who grew up in the fellowship of the United Societies and continued with them until over thirty years of age. Before he left them, he published a book, entitled "Plain Reasons", which set forth the Covenanters' grounds of dissent from the Revolution Church and State. Clarkson felt called to the Gospel ministry, and seeing no possibility of ordination among the Covenanters, he forsook them and joined the Seceders or Associate Presbytery, which had recently (1733) been organized.[18] The Associate Presbytery, before receiving him, required him to renounce his former Cameronian profession.[19] Patrick Walker took the trouble to attend the meeting of the Associate Presbytery to testify against Clarkson, that the latter had been joined with Macmillan in disowning the civil magistrate, but Clarkson's statements satisfied both Walker and the Associate Presbytery, which

---

[17] Morrison. George H., *Memoirs of the Life, Time, and Writings of the Reverend and Learned Thomas Boston, , A. M.*, p. 225, footnote.

[18] *Act, Declaration, and Testimony*, p. 154.

[19] Ibid.

received him as a candidate.[20] The United Societies were indignant at the action of the Associate Presbytery in requiring Clarkson to renounce Cameronian principles, and in 1741 they went on record to express their grief that "the Associate Presbytery have made subjection and loyalty to the present possessors of civil power a necessary term of communion... as was done in the case of Mr. Andrew Clarkson, who behoved to make an open renunciation of his former principles on that point before they would license him".[21]

During the period from the Revolution to the organization of the Reformed Presbytery in 1743 there existed a number of fragmentary dissenting parties, not connected with the United Societies but holding somewhat the same ground, which never attained an ecclesiastical organization. One of these was the Adamson party. Adamson was a licentiate of the Revolution Church. At one time he wished to join the United Societies, but they put him off until they could learn more about him and his principles, which offended Adamson. Patrick Walker says that Adamson was a man "on whose head the moon had influence, especially at its height; his publick letters to the Presbytery and Magistrates of Perth are a sufficient evidence of this".[22] Adamson then gathered disciples about himself and started a separate dissenting party. The Established Church excommunicated him, and he retaliated by excommunicating it.[23] Walker reports that a group of Christians concealed themselves in his premises and watched him for forty-eight

---

[20] Walker, *op. cit.*, II, pp. 235-236, quoting MS. Minutes of Associate Presbytery, 1733-1740, p. 304.

[21] Walker, *op. cit.* II, pp. 235-236, quoting *Declaration and Testimony* published at Mount-Herick, near Crawford-John, 1741, p. 39.

[22] Walker, *op. cit.*, I, p. 244.

[23] *Ibid.*, I, pp. 243-244.

hours, and noted that in all that time he did not once engage in prayer, whereupon they decided he was devoid of grace, and deserted him.[24] Adamson was not ordained, but did not hesitate to administer the sacrament of baptism. The followers of Adamson were commonly called Cameronians, but really were not, and Adamson preached strongly against Macmillan for disowning the civil magistrate.[25]

Two other fragmentary Covenanting parties outside the United Societies were the Harlites or Harleyites and the Howdenites or Howdonites. Patrick Walker states that these differed from each other and from Macmillan in some points, but that they agreed in disowning the Revolution State, separating from the Revolution Church and from all ministers who did not agree with them, and against paying all crown-dues.[26] The United Societies allowed payment of all ordinary taxes, while they protested against payment of the "cess" which had been a special tax levied to support the forces which persecuted the Covenanters before the Revolution. Walker states that the leaders of the Harleyite party were men "overdriven with enthusiastick quakerish notions, acted and led by John Gib's spirit, and Mr. Patrick Grant and some few with him", who had "been dotting with a dizzy head these 14 years, since I was in debate with him".[27] Walker adds that John and Andrew Harleys usurped the office of the ministry, to which they had not been properly called, and says "and yet all these are foolishly called Cameronians".[28] The Grant referred to was Peter or Patrick Grant, a man who had opposed James Renwick. In 1714 he published a pamphlet entitled "An Bond of Union wherein the Land's sins and

---

[24] *Ibid.*, I, pp. 244-245.

[25] *Ibid.*, II, p. 169, note 14.

[26] *Ibid.*, I, pp. 142-143.

[27] *Ibid.*, I, pp. 241-242.

[28] *Ibid.*

defections are discovered and witnessed against, also Truth vindicated and the Land's duty espoused...".[29] Walker states that in 1714 Grant's party numbered three men and three women, and that by 1724 they had increased to six men and six women.[30] In the "Bond of Union" they rejected King, government and Parliament, and repealed the acts which imposed the "cess" and other laws. They held that a mere passive dissent from the Revolution State was insufficient and inconsistent with Christian duty, and affirmed that "our will, inclinations and intentions are to change the form of government that has been in this land by monarchie", and "to set up a common-wealth government, the form and fabrick of which is a little touched at in the Smoking Flax".[31] For the time being they would confine the exercise of power to their own membership, while waiting for the Lord's appointed time to "exercise it in full extent over the adversary".[32] The existence during the post-Revolution period of these fanatical dissenting Covenanting sects no doubt explains the fact that the modern Reformed Presbyterian testimonies reject as an error the doctrine "that Christians are bound to take up arms in order to effect a change in the moral state of the nations",[33] or "that Christians, under pretence of hearing an active testimony, are bound to effect a change in the moral state of nations with the sword".[34]

In 1743 Thomas Nairne, a minister who had forsaken the Revolution Church to join the Associate Presbytery, left

[29] *Ibid.*, II, pp. 167-168.

[30] *Ibid.*

[31] *Ibid.*

[32] *Ibid.*

[33] *Testimony of the Reformed Presbyterian Church of Ireland*, Part 1 (Doctrinal And Practical), p. 116.

[34] *Reformation Principles Exhibited by the Reformed Presbyterian Church in the United States of America*, p. 244.

the latter to join the United Societies. Nairne was in agreement with Macmillan, and his doctrine of the civil magistrate caused his breach with the Seceders. The Ploughlandhead Testimony witnesses against the Associate Presbytery because the latter excommunicated Nairne for his views on civil government, and adds: "although, in adorable providence, he has since been left to fall into the practice of such immorality, as has justly rendered him the object of church censure by this presbytery", that is, by the Reformed Presbytery.[35]

The accession of Nairne to the United Societies opened the way for the constitution of the Reformed Presbytery, which was done on August 1st, 1743, at Braehead, by Macmillan, Nairne and ruling elders.[36] The General Meetings of the United Societies continued for several years after this, but all ecclesiastical functions were in the hands of the Presbytery.[37] All the minutes of the Reformed Presbytery from 1743 to 1758 are lost, and the only sources of information about the actions of the presbytery during that period are pamphlets, letters, and the minutes of other judicatories.[38]

In 1745 the Covenants were renewed at Auchensaugh, and the sacrament of the Lord's Supper was administered at the same time. Some of the communion tokens used on that occasion, bearing the letters "G M" (General Meeting) are still in existence.[39]

From 1744 to 1751 five young men were licensed to

---

[35] *Act, Declaration, and Testimony*, p. 157.

[36] Hutchison, *op. cit.*, p. 187.

[37] *Ibid.*, p. 189.

[38] *Ibid.*, p. 190.

[39] *Ibid.*

preach and ordained to the office of the ministry by the Reformed Presbytery.[40] Among these was John Cuthbertson, who went to America and in 1774 was one of the constituent members of the first American Reformed Presbytery, which in 1782 united with the American Associate Presbytery to form the Associate Reformed Church, the majority of which in 1858 united with the Associate Synod of North America to become the United Presbyterian Church of North America.

3.   The Division of the Reformed Presbytery, 1753.

In 1749 Thomas Mair, a Seceder minister, published a posthumous book by the Rev. James Fraser, minister of the Revolution Church who had died in 1698. The book was entitled "A Treatise on Justifying Faith", and sets forth a doctrine of universal atonement which is essentially Arminian or Amyraldian. Mair himself adopted some of the views in the book, and was deposed from the ministry.[41] James Walker, in "The Theology and Theologians of Scotland" (1872) summarizes Fraser's views as follows (pp.48-49): "He asserts 'that Christ obeyed and died in the room of all as the representative of fallen man;' that 'men are all fundamentally justified in Him and through Him'. 'That Christ died for all'. But, then, are all men saved? No; God did not mean to save any but His chosen. What, then, was the effect of that one indivisible sacrifice for all which God's Son offered on the cross? Well, first of all, to lay a real foundation for the Gospel offer. For every man was satisfaction rendered, and every man might appropriate it as something subjectively real. Is it simply the old story of a conditional salvation? Not at all. Fraser scorns the notion of conditional redemption and salvation. Men take, he says, low

---

[40] *Ibid.*

[41] *Ibid.*, p. 194.

and insufficient views of the Saviour's work when they think it had respect to human happiness alone. The manifestation of God's justice and grace is its last and highest end. And this, according to him, is the glory of His scheme. It lays a basis for the Gospel in which reprobates as well as the elect can be asked to believe, while they are not, as the elect, brought under a divine appointment unto life; and hence, too, it follows that, in their free rejection of what is simple verity, they become liable, not to law, but to gospel wrath and vengeance; and the same blood which magnifies God's grace exceedingly, magnifies essentially His justice. It comes to this, in short, Fraser plainly states it, that Christ dies for reprobates that they may come under a more tremendous doom; as, on the other hand, he dies for the elect that theirs may be an all-transcendent blessedness".[42]

After the publication of this book, some of the ministers of the Reformed Presbytery adopted part of the views advocated in it. They did not accept all that was taught in the book, but they did accept the doctrine of the universal atonement. The Reformed Presbytery had been organized less than ten years, and now heresy appeared and nearly wrecked the enterprise. Those members of the Reformed Presbytery who accepted the doctrine of the universal atonement maintained that Christ's satisfaction was "clothed with a two-fold divine appointment, the one general, the other special. In the former sense Christ satisfied for the sins of all mankind, so that His satisfaction may be sustained as the legal ground and meritorious cause for which mankind should be admitted into a state of probation, declared capable of receiving an offer of life and of salvation, and upon which they should be authorized to rest and plead for their deliverance from their guilt and misery. On the other hand, the satisfaction of Christ as clothed with a special appointment, is the legal ground and

---

[42] *Ibid.*, p. 195.

meritorious cause for which a chosen number of mankind shall certainly be saved".[43]   These men also "held that common benefits, enjoyed by reprobates as well as by the elect, were the purchase of Christ by his death".[44]   The Reformed Presbytery denied the two-fold significance of the atonement, and also the doctrine that Christ by his death purchased common benefits for the reprobate, and held that the benefits enjoyed by the reprobate "are rather to be accounted consequents following upon Christ's Purchase than proper Effects thereof as to them".[45]

In 1749 the Reformed Presbytery adopted four propositions against the doctrines of Fraser's book, one of which was "That the Lord Jesus Christ represented and died upon the cross only in the room and stead of a select number of mankind".[46]   James Hall, one of the newly ordained ministers, led the party in the Reformed Presbytery that held the novel views of the atonement. Macmillan was ill and unable to attend the meeting of the Reformed Presbytery in the fall of 1752, but sent a letter to the court warning against the doctrines of Fraser's book. It was decided to take the matter up formally at the spring meeting of 1753. When that meeting was held, four ministers and five elders were present.   Nairne was under censure, and had left the Reformed Presbyterian Church, and Cuthbertson had gone to America.[47]   After considerable debate, a proposition was formulated to be voted on, as follows: "Whether Mr. Fraser's maintaining that the Lord Jesus Christ satisfied for the sins of all mankind, so that His satisfaction may be competent to be proposed to them in the gospel, and pleaded by them for their

---

[43] *Ibid.*, p. 196.

[44] *Ibid.*, p. 197.

[45] *Ibid.*

[46] *Ibid.*, pp. 197-198.

[47] *Ibid.*

justification; and that this satisfaction is the Ground and Formal Reason upon which faith is founded, be a dangerous doctrine?"[48] When the vote was taken, the doctrine was declared dangerous by a vote of five to three. MacMillan and his son and three of the elders voted to condemn the doctrine as dangerous; Hall and the other two elders voted on the other side. Innes, the Moderator, did not vote, but agreed with the minority.[49]

The matter had apparently been settled by a majority vote, but the worst was yet to come. The following day the minority attempted to have the decision reversed, but failed. Hall then handed in a paper in his own name and the name of those who adhered to him, in which he took the ground that the decision was not binding because two members had been absent, and because it was contrary to an important doctrine of the Christian religion. After this the minority asked the presbytery to suspend the majority from the ministry and eldership, which was certainly an astonishing demand. While part of those who had voted with the majority were temporarily away from the meeting, the minority hastily adjourned the court and immediately made their escape, taking with them the minutes and records of the Reformed Presbytery, which from that day to this have never been recovered.[50]

The ministers and elders who had left the Reformed Presbytery in this precipitous fashion constituted a judicatory which they called the Reformed Presbytery of Edinburgh. They issued a pamphlet entitled "A True State of the Difference", which was filled with aspersions upon the character and activities of the senior Macmillan. In 1754 the

---

[48] *Ibid.*

[49] *Ibid.*

[50] *Ibid.*, p. 199.

Reformed Presbytery published a pamphlet entitled "A Serious Examination", which vindicated Macmillan's name, and was sanctioned by the presbytery. It was supposed to have been written by Macmillan, junior.[51]

The Reformed Presbytery of Edinburgh grew for a time, and ordained a number of ministers. Soon, however, they were torn apart by dissensions among themselves. From the origin of their organization, some of them had rejected parts of the Westminster Confession of Faith and part of the Informatory Vindication.[52] Hall died in 1798. The presbytery continued to hold meetings until 1817, but appears to have dissolved soon after that date.[53]

Hutchison states that there is reason to believe that some of the party which organized the Reformed Presbytery of Edinburgh later became members of the first Unitarian congregation formed in Edinburgh.[54] The Ploughlandhead Testimony of 1761 mentions the division of 1753 and condemns it in the following terms: "Again, the presbytery find themselves in duty obliged to testify against these brethren who some time ago have broken off from their communion, for their unwarrantable separation, and continued opposition to the truth and testimony, in the hands of this presbytery, even to the extent of presuming, in a judicial capacity, to threaten church censure against the presbytery, without alleging so much as any other reason for this strange procedure, than their refusing to approve as truth, a point of doctrine, that stands condemned by the standards of the Reformed Church of *Scotland*, founded on the

---

[51] *Ibid.*, p. 200.

[52] *Ibid.*, p. 201.

[53] *Ibid.*

[54] *Ibid.*

authority of divine revelation "[55] The Testimony continues at some length to review the conduct of Hall, Innes and their party after the division, alleging that they adopted "a loose and latitudinarian scheme of principles, on the point of church communion".[56]

This controversy is reflected in the Declaration and Testimony of the Reformed Presbyterian Church of North America, which rejects as an error the doctrine "That Christ purchased any benefit for the reprobate".[57]

In 1761 the Reformed Presbytery adopted its first judicial Testimony, at Ploughlandhead. The full title of the document is *Act, Declaration, and Testimony for the Whole of our Covenanted Reformation, as Attained to, and Established in, Britain and Ireland; Particularly Betwixt the Years 1638 and 1649, Inclusive. As, also, Against all the Steps of Defection from said Reformation, Whether in Former or Later Times, since the Overthrow of that Glorious Work, Down to this Present Day: By the Reformed Presbytery.* [58] The preparation of this document had been contemplated earlier, but was delayed for several years by the controversy about the doctrine of the atonement.[59] From 1761 on acceptance of the Ploughlandhead Testimony was required as a condition of membership in the Reformed

---

[55] *Act, Declaration, and Testimony*, pp. 157-158.

[56] *Ibid.*, p. 158.

[57] *Reformation Principles Exhibited by the Reformed Presbyterian Church in the United States of America*, Part II (Declaration and Testimony), Chapter X, Error 7, p. 176.

[58] Johnston, op. cit., pp. 163-164; the Ploughlandhead Testimony was republished in Philadelphia, 1876, with additions and notes by the "Reformed Presbytery", i.e., the Covenanted Reformed Presbyterian Church, which originated in the separation of the Rev. David Steele et al. from the Reformed Presbyterian Synod, Pittsburgh 1840.

[59] *Testimony of the Reformed Presbyterian Church of Ireland*, Part II (Historical), p. 112.

Presbyterian Church, until 1837 when the new Testimony appeared.[60] The 1761 Testimony is an elaborate document of some 75,000 words, of a historical and argumentative nature, to really understand and intelligently accept which must have required a knowledge of history far greater than is common among intelligent Christians today; indeed the requirement that applicants for membership profess acceptance of such a long and complicated document must have been a temptation to many to profess acceptance by an implicit faith. The Testimony was amended and reprinted in 1762, 1777, 1797 and 1818.[61] The new Testimony was composed of two distinct parts, a doctrinal and a historical, the former of which was published in 1837 and the latter in 1839.[62]

In 1810 the Reformed Presbytery was sub-divided into three presbyteries, Northern, Southern and Eastern, and in 1811 the first Synod of the Reformed Presbyterian Church of Scotland was constituted.[63]

4. The Division of the Reformed Presbyterian Synod, 1863.

From its origin to 1863 the Reformed Presbyterian Church had maintained the principle of political dissent from the British constitution. In 1863 a controversy arose over the question of the elective franchise. The Synod which was held in that year adopted the following motion: "The Synod, having read the reports from Presbyteries and Sessions anent taking the oath of allegiance and exercising the elective franchise, find that all the Presbyteries and a majority of Sessions, confining themselves to the consideration of the

---

[60] *Ibid.*, Johnston, op. cit., pp. 163-164.

[61] Johnston, *op. cit.*, pp. 163-164.

[62] *Ibid.*

[63] *Summary of the Testimony of the Reformed Presbyterian Church of Scotland*, p. 36.

point of exercise of discipline for the acts therein specified, have adopted said overture only to this extent. The Synod, therefore, in accordance with these reports enacts that, while recommending the members of the Church to abstain from the use of the franchise and from taking the oath of allegiance, discipline to the effect of suspension and expulsion from the privileges of the Church shall cease, and earnestly enjoin upon all under their charge to have respect to this decision, and to follow after the things which make for peace, and things whereby one may edify another".[64] This was equivalent to abandoning the position of political dissent, so far as the Church as such was concerned, and leaving it an open question for every member to decide for himself. On May 7th, 1863, the minority filed with the Synod a protest, signed by the Rev. W. Anderson and others, which stated: "We, the undersigned ministers and elders, members of the Synod of the Reformed Presbyterian Church in Scotland, in our own name, and in the name of all adhering to us, do hereby protest against the decision now adopted as the law of the Church by the majority of this court, as opposed to the Word of God, and to the Testimony of the Church, and unconstitutionally adopted; and seeing that they have thereby abandoned, in regard to the matters referred to in that decision, the principles of the Reformed Presbyterian Church clearly set forth in her Testimony, to which we are all solemnly pledged, and have thereby departed from the Scriptural position which the Church has occupied for more than 170 years; we do hereby protest and claim for ourselves, and for those adhering to us, to be constitutionally the Synod of the Reformed Presbyterian Church in Scotland", etc.[65] This was signed by three ministers and four elders.[66] These continued their organization as a separate Synod, maintaining

---

[64] Johnston, *op. cit.*, p. 164.

[65] *Ibid.*

[66] *Ibid.*

what had been the principles of the whole body before 1863.[67]

5.   The Union of the Larger Reformed Presbyterian Synod with the Free Church, 1876.

In 1863 negotiations were begun for the organic union of various Presbyterian bodies in Scotland. The negotiations broke on the rock of the question of the relation of the civil magistrate to the Church and to religion, and were abandoned in 1873.[68] Before the breach occurred, a report was made by the Committee which had conducted the negotiations. This report, dated May, 1873, lists articles on which the various parties were agreed, and also articles which were not agreed upon, but which were distinctive of various Presbyterian bodies. The Churches involved were the Presbyterian Church of England, the Free Church of Scotland, the United Presbyterian Church of Scotland, and the Reformed Presbyterian Church (larger body). Among the articles which were agreed upon were the following: 1. It was agreed that civil government is an ordinance of God, and that the magistrate like other men must be subject to Christ, and must regulate his conduct according to Scripture. 2. That the civil magistrate ought to be a Christian, and ought in his official capacity to publicly further the Christian religion, and to be ruled by it in making laws, administering justice, swearing oaths, etc. 3. That it is not within the province of the civil magistrate to impose a creed or form of worship on his subjects, or interfere with the government of the Church, "It being the exclusive prerogative of the Lord Jesus to rule in matters of faith and worship". 4. Marriage, the Sabbath, and the appointment of days of national humiliation and thanksgiving, are practical instances to which these principles

---

[67] *Summary of the Testimony of the Reformed Presbyterian Church of Scotland*, p. 36.

[68] Johnston, *op. cit.*, pp. 217-221.

apply. 5. "That the Church and the State, being ordinances of God distinct from each other, they are capable of existing without either of them intruding into the proper province of the other, and ought not so to intrude. Erastian supremacy of the State over the Church, and Anti-christian domination of the Church over the State, ought to be condemned; and all schemes of connection involving or tending to either are, therefore, to be avoided. The Church has a spiritual authority over such of the subjects and rulers of earthly kingdoms as are in her communion, and the civil powers have the same secular authority over the members and office-bearers of the Church as over the rest of their subjects. The Church has no power over earthly kingdoms in their collective and civil capacity, nor have they any power over her as a Church. But, though thus distinct, the Church and the State owe mutual duties to each other, and acting within their respective spheres, may be signally subservient to each other's welfare". 6."That the Church cannot lawfully surrender or compromise her spiritual independence for any worldly consideration or advantage whatsoever. And further, the Church must ever maintain the essential and perpetual obligation which Christ has laid on all His people, to support and extend His Church by free-will offerings".[69]

The distinctive articles presented by the Reformed Presbyterian Committee were as follows: "1. While friendly alliance ought always to be kept in view as the normal relation of the Church and state, the question whether, or to what extent, the realization of it in any given case ought to be attempted, cannot lawfully or safely be determined without taking into account the circumstances, character, and attainments of both; particularly the degree of unity which the Church has attained, and the extent to which the State has become Christian. 2. While the Church is bound to uphold

[69] *Ibid.*

civil government, founded on right principles, and directed to its appropriate ends, nevertheless, as a public witness for the truth and claims of Christ, it ought to testify against whatever is immoral in the civil constitution, or iniquitous in public policy. 3. When the Civil magistrate sets himself in habitual opposition to, and abuses his power for the overturning of religion and the national liberties, he thereby forfeits his right to conscientious allegiance, especially in countries where religion and liberty have been placed under the protection of a righteous constitution. 4. While it is not lawful for the magistrate to grant aid to the Church from the national resources, merely from motives of political expediency, it is competent for the Church to accept aid from those resources, provided that the terms in which it is given do not involve the Church in approbation of that which is evil in the constitution of the State; but the national resources cannot lawfully be employed for the support of truth and error indiscriminately".[70]

The Original Secession Magazine, commenting on the foregoing, spoke as follows: "It is not altogether unnoticeable here that the Reformed Presbyterian Synod's Committee, though the representatives of those who so long claimed to be Covenanters, *par excellence* , has entirely ignored the Covenants, and the doctrine of covenant obligation, in their statement of principles given in to the Joint-Committee. In acting thus they have the credit of adopting a wise and consistent policy. For, to human view (though with God all things are possible) they might about as soon expect to remove the Alps from their present basis by any lever power which they could employ, as raise the United Presbyterian Church and the Free to the platform of the Second Reformation, and an advocacy and avouchment of the Covenants; and to lift up a testimony for their continued

[70] *Ibid.*

obligation and against the perjury of the Church and kingdom in the manifold violation of these solemn deeds, and virtual repudiation of their obligation".[71]

The negotiations failed, as the divergent views held by the Churches involved proved to be irreconcilable. They show, however, the desire for union which existed at that time and which resulted in the union of two of the bodies involved in 1876. These were the Free Church, which had originated in the Disruption of the Established Church in 1843, and the larger of the two Reformed Presbyterian Synods. On May 25th, 1876, at Edinburgh, the two bodies entered into organic union. Seventy ministers and elders, representing the Reformed Presbyterian Synod, dissolved their judicatory to unite with the Free Church.[72] Only one congregation of the larger Reformed Presbyterian Synod elected to remain out of this union.[73] This left the smaller of the two bodies into which the original Reformed Presbyterian Synod had divided in 1863 to continue alone as the legitimate continuation and spiritual succession of the followers of Cameron, Cargill, Renwick and Macmillan. The Free Church, with which the larger body united in 1876, united with the United Presbyterian Church to form the United Free Church in 1900, and the United Free Church united with the Established Church in 1929, so that the Reformed Presbyterians who adhered to the larger Synod in 1863, in 1929 found themselves in organic union with the Established Church of Scotland, after 239 years of dissent from that body, from 1690 to 1929.

The smaller of the two bodies resulting from the division of 1863 continues to the present day as the Reformed

---

[71] *Ibid.*, p. 220.

[72] *Ibid.*, pp. 230-234.

[73] Horne, C. Silvester, *A Popular History of the Free Churches*, p. 386.

Presbyterian Church of Scotland. The following is a brief statement of the present distinctive position of that Church, as found in the "Summary of the Testimony of the Reformed Presbyterian Church of Scotland", published by the Synod in 1932: "The great cardinal truths of the Gospel are professed not only by the various Churches, great and small, into which Presbyterian Scotland is divided, but also by other evangelical denominations. They teach that the Son of God died for sinners and that salvation is free to all who will repent and believe on Him.

"It is the duty of Christ's Church, however, to confess all His truth, and to observe all things whatsoever He has commanded. Under this conviction Reformed Presbyterians, while joyfully esteeming other Christians as brethren in the Lord, abide by the distinctive doctrines and practices which they have been taught to regard as in accordance with the Scripture and the mind of Christ. For this reason they cannot conscientiously surrender their separate position as a Church, which is the indispensable organ of their testimony.

"Of the various sections of Scottish Presbyterians, none has ever proposed to stand with the Reformed Presbyterians on the ground of political dissent. They alone as a denomination divest themselves of responsibility for the denial by all our present-day Parliamentary parties of Christ's claim to national obedience. They are the only religious body in Scotland who maintain that one cannot be true to Christ as Lawgiver and King of Nations and at the same time be a party to the present British Constitution or give their vote to Parliamentary candidates who accept that Constitution. As believers in the Headship of Christ and in the Covenants of our fore-fathers, we cannot help to place in power parties or persons who avow the political principle that atheists, agnostics, Romanists and other enemies of the Protestant faith are entitled to sit in the Legislature and hold places of power and trust in the government of this professedly Protestant Nation".[74]

---

[74] *Summary of the Testimony of the Reformed Presbyterian Church of Scotland*, pp. 38-39.

PART III

THE DISTINCTIVE DOCTRINES OF THE COVENANTERS

CHAPTER I

THE CONTINUING OBLIGATION OF THE SCOTTISH COVENANTS

1. The Origin of Covenanting at the First Reformation.

The earliest religious covenant of which we have a record in Scotland was a "Band" made in 1556 by the "gentlemen of Mearns" under the leadership of John Knox.[1] What is commonly called "The First Covenant" as made in 1557, and was a mutual bond for the renunciation of Popery and the defence of the Gospel.[2] The "Second Covenant" or "Band for Mutual Defence" was signed at Perth, May 31st, 1559.[3] This was followed by the "Third Covenant", which was signed at Stirling on August 1st of the same year.[4] The "Fourth Covenant" or "Band for Expelling the French" was signed at Edinburgh, April 27th, 1560.[5] In 1562 the "Fifth Band" was signed by the "Barons and Gentlemen" of Kyle, Carrick and Cunningham.[6] The "Sixth Covenant" was signed by the citizens of Edinburgh in 1572.[7] From these facts it

---

[1] Johnston, John C., *Treasury of the Scottish Covenant*. p. 23.

[2] *Ibid.*, p. 24.

[3] *Ibid.*, p. 25.

[4] *Ibid.*, p. 26.

[5] *Ibid.*, p. 27.

[6] *Ibid.*

[7] *Ibid.*

will be seen that the godly in Scotland, from the beginning of
the Reformation, adopted the practice of signing covenants or
"bands" for mutual protection and for the defence of
Protestantism.

The first covenant of epoch making significance in
Scotland was the National Covenant, which was written in
1580. The occasion for this covenant was the public fear of
Jesuit plots and attempts to restore Popery and destroy the
Reformation. At the request of King James VI the document
was written by John Craig, an Edinburgh minister.[8] It was
first signed by the King and his household, in 1580, and then
by persons of all ranks in Scotland in 1581.[9] It was again
signed by all classes in 1590.[10] It became the basis of the
National Covenant as adopted in 1638, in which year it was
signed in its new form by great numbers of people, as it was
again in 1639.[11] In the form drawn up in 1638, it was
ratified by the General Assembly in 1638 and again in 1639,
and by an act of Parliament in 1640, and was accepted by
King Charles II at Spey in 1650 and at Scone on his
coronation, January 1st, 1651.[12]

The Solemn League and Covenant was drafted by
Alexander Henderson, and approved by the General
Assembly of the Church of Scotland in August, 1643. It was
then sent to England, where it was adopted and sworn by the
House of Commons and the Westminster Assembly of
Divines jointly. After this it was sent back to Scotland, where

---

[8] *Testimony of the Reformed Presbyterian Church of Ireland*, Part II
(Historical), p. 41.

[9] Heading or sub-title of the National Covenant, as printed in many editions
of the Westminster Standards.

[10] *Ibid.*

[11] *Ibid.*

[12] *Ibid.*

it was signed and sworn by the Commission of the General Assembly and by the Committee of Estates of the Parliament. It was distributed throughout Scotland and signed with great unanimity by all classes of people excepting those who favored Popery or Prelacy. With an "Acknowledgment of Sins, and Engagement to Duties" it was again sworn by all ranks in Scotland in 1648, and by the Parliament in 1649. Finally, it was subscribed by King Charles II at Spey in 1650, and on the occasion of his coronation at Scone, New Year's Day, 1651.[13]

2.   Analysis of the Covenants of 1580, 1638 and 1643.

The National Covenant as adopted in 1580, sometimes called the "King's Confession" or "Confession of Faith", is a document of about 1,000 words. It is a profession of faith in the Gospel, of acceptance of the Scots Confession of Faith (1560), and a renunciation of the whole Roman Catholic system, which is plainly called Antichrist. It contains a very long and full list of the errors and abuses of Romanism, all of which are condemned and rejected in no uncertain terms. The Covenant opens thus: "We all and every one of us under-written, protest, That, after long and due examination of our own consciences in matters of true and false religion, we are now thoroughly resolved in the truth by the word and Spirit of God: and therefore we believe with our hearts, confess with our mouths, subscribe with our hands, and constantly affirm, before God and the whole world, that this only is the true Christian faith and religion, pleasing God, and bringing salvation to man, which now is, by the mercy of God, revealed to the world by the preaching of the blessed evangel"... The Covenant closes with an oath to

---

[13] Heading or sub-title of the Solemn League and Covenant as printed in many editions of the Westminster Standards.

defend the person and authority of the King "in the defence of Christ his evangel, liberties of our country, ministration of justice, and punishment of iniquity, against all enemies within this realm or without, as we desire our God to be a strong and merciful defender to us in the day of our death, and coming of our Lord Jesus Christ; to whom, with the Father, and the Holy Spirit, be all honour and glory eternally. Amen".

When the National Covenant was renewed in 1638 it consisted of three parts. The first of these was the Covenant of 1580 *verbatim* . The second was a legal section, which was prepared by Archibald Johnston, who later became Lord Wariston. This section lists a large number of acts of former Parliaments which are cited to prove that the course taken in adopting and renewing the Covenant was not illegal or unconstitutional, but in harmony with the law of the land. The third part was prepared by Alexander Henderson and constituted the application of the Covenant to the conditions existing in 1638. This part contains a rejection of Prelacy, of "novations" or corruptions in the worship of God, and of the civil places and power of kirkmen, "till they be tried and allowed in free Assemblies and in Parliament".   The innovations in the government and worship of the Church are rejected as having no warrant in Scripture, contrary to the Scots Confession of Faith, contrary to "the intention and meaning of the blessed reformers of religion in this land", and contrary to the acts of Parliament which had been enumerated in the second part of the Covenant. The third part continues: "And therefore, from the knowledge and conscience of our duty to God, to our King and country, without any worldly respect or inducement, so far as human infirmity will suffer, wishing a farther measure of the grace of God for this effect; we promise and swear, by the GREAT NAME OF THE LORD OUR GOD, to continue in the profession and obedience of the foresaid religion; and that we shall defend the same, and resist all these contrary errors and corruptions, according to our vocation, and to the uttermost of that power that God hath put in our hands, all the days of our life". After this comes a qualified pledge to support and defend the King: "we promise and swear, That we shall, to the uttermost of our power, with our means and lives, stand to the defence of our dread Sovereign the King's Majesty, his person and authority, in the defence and preservation of the foresaid true religion, liberties, and laws of the kingdom; as also to the mutual defence and assistance every one of us of another, in the same cause of maintaining the true religion, and his Majesty's authority, with our best counsel, our bodies, means, and whole power, against all sorts of persons whatsoever; so that whatsoever shall be done to the least of us for that cause, shall be taken as done to us all in general, and to every one of us in particular". The Covenant closes with a promise to accompany a covenanted profession with a godly life, and with a call for "the LIVING GOD, THE SEARCHER OF OUR HEARTS, to witness, who knoweth this to be our sincere desire and unfeigned resolution, as we shall answer to JESUS CHRIST in the great day, and under the pain of God's everlasting wrath, and of infamy and loss of all honour and respect in this world; most humbly beseeching the LORD to strengthen us by his HOLY SPIRIT for this end, and to bless our desires and proceedings with a happy success; that religion and righteousness may flourish in the land, to the glory of GOD, the honour of our King, and peace and comfort of us all. In witness whereof, we have subscribed with our hands all the premises".

The Solemn League and Covenant consists of an introductory paragraph, six articles and a concluding paragraph. The introduction reads: "We Noblemen, Barons, Knights, Gentlemen, Citizens, Burgesses, Ministers of the

Gospel, and Commons of all sorts, in the kingdoms of Scotland. England, and Ireland, by the providence of GOD, living under one King, and being of one reformed religion, having before our eyes the glory of GOD, and the advancement of the kingdom of our Lord and Saviour JESUS CHRIST, the honour and happiness of the King's Majesty, and his posterity, and the true public liberty, safety, and peace of the kingdoms, wherein every one's private condition is included: And calling to mind the treacherous and bloody plots, conspiracies, attempts, and practices of the enemies of GOD, against the true religion and professors thereof in all places, especially in these three kingdoms, ever since the reformation of religion; and how much their rage, power, and presumption are of late, and at this time, increased and exercised, whereof the deplorable state of the church and kingdom of Ireland, the distressed estate of the church and kingdom of England, and the dangerous estate of the church and kingdom of Scotland, are present and public testimonies; we have now at last, (after other means of supplication and remonstrance, protestation, and sufferings) for the preservation of ourselves and our religion from utter ruin and destruction, according to the commendable practice of these kingdoms in former times, and the example of GOD'S people in other nations, after mature deliberation, resolved and determined to enter into a mutual and solemn League and Covenant, wherein we all subscribe, and each one of us for himself, with our hands lifted up to the most High GOD, do swear."

Article I binds the swearers to endeavor the preservation of the Reformed religion in Scotland, in doctrine, worship, discipline and government, the reformation of religion in England and Ireland, in doctrine, worship, discipline and government, "according to the Word of God, and the example of the best reformed Churches", and to endeavor to bring the Churches in the three kingdoms to the nearest possible uniformity "in religion, confession of faith, form of church-government, directory for worship and catechising".

Article II binds the swearers to endeavor, without respect of persons, the "extirpation" of Popery, Prelacy, superstition, heresy, schism, profaneness, "and whatsoever shall be found to be contrary to sound doctrine and the power of godliness".

Article III binds the swearers to endeavor with their estates and lives, to preserve the rights and privileges of the Parliaments, and the liberties of the kingdoms, "and to preserve and defend the King's Majesty's person and authority, in the preservation and defence of the true religion, and liberties of the kingdoms; that the world may bear witness with our consciences of our loyalty, and that we have no thoughts or intentions to diminish his Majesty's just power and greatness".

Article IV binds the swearers to "endeavour the discovery of all such as have been or shall be incendiaries, malignants, or evil instruments, by hindering the reformation of religion, dividing the King from his people, or one of the kingdoms from another, or making any faction or parties amongst the people, contrary to this League and Covenant; that they may be brought to public trial, and receive condign punishment", etc.

Article V binds the swearers to endeavor that the three kingdoms "may remain conjoined in a firm peace and union to all posterity; and that justice may be done upon the wilful opposers thereof", etc.

Article VI binds the swearers to mutual assistance, and not to suffer themselves "directly or indirectly, by whatsoever combination, persuasion, or terror, to be divided and withdrawn from this blessed union and conjunction, whether to make defection to the contrary part, or to give ourselves to a detestable indifferency and neutrality, in this cause, which so much concerneth the glory of GOD, the good of the kingdom, and honour of the King", etc.

The concluding paragraph of the Solemn League and Covenant contains a confession of sins and promise of amendment, and ends with the words: "And this Covenant we make in the presence of ALMIGHTY GOD, the Searcher of all hearts, with a true intention to perform the same, as we shall answer at that great day, when the secrets of all hearts shall be disclosed; most humbly beseeching the Lord to strengthen us by his HOLY SPIRIT for this end, and to bless our desires and proceedings with such success, as may be deliverance and safety to his people, and encouragement to other Christian churches, groaning under, or in danger of, the yoke of antichristian tyranny, to join in the same or like association and covenant, to the glory of GOD, the enlargement of the kingdom of JESUS CHRIST, and the peace and tranquillity of Christian kingdoms and commonwealths".

The Solemn League and Covenant was a very definite engagement. In the first instance it was binding on the individual swearers and subscribers: "We all subscribe, and each one of us for himself", etc. Being formally adopted by the Parliaments of England and Scotland, as well as by the Church of Scotland and the Westminster Assembly, it became binding on the nations as such. Lastly, as it was subscribed by Charles II on the occasion of his coronation, it became binding on him, not only in his private capacity as a man, but in his official capacity as King. The content of the document is also very definite; its six articles are brief and to the point. The only point left somewhat unclear is in Article I, where it is stated that the swearers bind themselves to endeavor the reformation of religion in England and Ireland, according to the Word of God, and the example of the best reformed Churches. This does not state which Churches were the best reformed Churches, but it appears to have been generally understood at the time that the Church of Scotland and the Continental Churches holding the Calvinistic faith and Presbyterian system of government were meant.

It will be seen at once that in addition to what is stated in the Solemn League and Covenant, something is presupposed. The Covenant takes for granted that there is to be but one Church in each of the three kingdoms, that that church is to be by law established, and that no other Church can be tolerated within the territorial limits of the kingdoms. Indeed, Article II expressly binds the swearers to the "extirpation", not only of Popery and Prelacy, but also of heresy and schism, that is, of all dissent from the legally established Church. The Reformed Presbyterian Church of Scotland still adheres to the Solemn League and Covenant, and holds that it is binding on the Church and nation, but that the word "extirpation" is not to be taken as involving force or violence.[14] When we remember that it was almost universally believed at that time that it is the duty of the civil magistrate to suppress schism and heresy,[15] and that the Solemn League and Covenant was taken by the Parliaments of England and Scotland, and not merely by religious bodies, it is difficult to believe that "extirpation" meant anything milder than legal suppression enforced by the power of the civil magistrate.

---

[14] *Summary of the Testimony of the Reformed Presbyterian Church of Scotland*, p. 28.

[15] Westminster Confession of Faith, XX. 4; XXIII. 3.

The sense put upon the word by the Reformed Presbyterian Church of Scotland today is doubtless far more compatible with sound principles than the original sense, but it is historically less accurate. Probably no adherent of the Covenants today believes that schism and heresy should be "extirpated" by any other method than persuasion, but that is certainly not the natural and proper meaning of the Solemn League and Covenant.

3.   Do the Covenants Purport to be Perpetually Binding?

The National Covenant as subscribed in 1580 and 1581 technically binds only the actual subscribers: "We all and every one of us under-written, protest ...that we shall continue in the obedience of the doctrine and discipline of this kirk, and shall defend the same, according to our vocation and power, all the days of our lives...". The National Covenant as renewed in 1638 contained the following statement: "And finally, being convinced in our minds, and confessing with our mouths, that the present and succeeding generations in this land are bound to keep the foresaid national oath and subscription inviolable...we... do hereby profess", etc. This shows that the National Covenant of 1638 purported to be inviolable and perpetually binding on the nation to all generations.

The Solemn League and Covenant purports to bind only the actual subscribers: "We Noblemen, Barons, Knights, Gentlemen, Citizens, Burgesses, Ministers of the Gospel, and Commons of all sorts...all subscribe, and each one of us for himself, with our hands lifted up to the most High GOD, do swear", etc. Article I, however, contains a statement which shows that the Solemn League and Covenant was intended to be a permanent and not merely a temporary arrangement: "that we, and our posterity after us, may, as brethren, live in faith and love, and the Lord may delight to dwell in the midst of us". Article V binds the swearers to endeavor that the three kingdoms "may remain conjoined in a firm peace and union to all posterity" which indicates that the religious oath sworn was intended to be perpetually binding upon the three kingdoms.

4.   The Perpetual Obligation of the Covenants as held by the Early Covenanters.

Samuel Rutherford held that "to pass in silence over the sworn Covenant" was no less than a denial of Christianity itself.[16] The Marquis of Argyle, in his speech on the scaffold in 1661, spoke thus: "But whatever they (Gallios) think, God hath laid engagements upon Scotland; we are tied by Covenant to religion and Reformation. Those that were then unborn are engaged to it, and in our baptism we are engaged to it, and it passes the power of any under heaven to absolve a man from the oath of God; they deceive themselves, and it may be will deceive others that think otherwise".[17]   A few days later James Guthrie was hanged, and in his speech on the scaffold he stated that no person or power on earth could loose or dispense the Covenants, that they were still binding on the three kingdoms, and would be forever hereafter. His last words were: "The Covenants, the Covenants, shall yet be Scotland's reviving".[18]

A sermon preached in 1663 by John Guthrie, minister at Tarbolton, sets forth with great fulness the arguments then in use by the Covenanters to prove the perpetual obligation of the Covenants. His text was Ezekiel 17:19, and his theme

---

[16] Stanley, Arthur Penrhyn, *Lectures on the History of the Church of Scotland, Delivered in Edinburgh in 1872*, p. 85.

[17] Johnston, *op. cit.*, p. 403.

[18] Ibid., p. 323.

was the indissoluble tie of the Covenant: "And lest any of you, who sometimes have heard us press the oath of the covenant in these lands, should now-a-days think it alterable, and look upon it as a thing to be dispensed with, we are, through God's strength, from Scripture, to make out the indissoluble tie of the Covenant". The text presupposes, but does not explicitly state, says Guthrie, that "every oath and covenant of God, is a thing inviolable, that is, may not and cannot be broken". He continues that he is not speaking of the covenant of works, nor of the covenant of grace, either in its old or new dispensation, because these covenants were devised by God. "But we take the covenants in this place, to be of men's duties in the land; and for keeping them the better, we take an oath upon us in things that are neither morally evil nor good but indifferent. But a man once engaged by oath cannot retract. Though they be not commanded duties, yet once entered into, they must stand, for when we open our mouths to the Lord we cannot go back". He continues, three things are necessary to an oath or covenant of God. 1. It must be a thing in itself lawful. 2. It must be a thing in itself possible, within man's power. 3. It must be taken in the name of the Lord. He next cites Scripture proofs to show that an oath is binding; then, that the inviolableness of an oath is "founded upon the law of nature and nations"; then he cites Scripture to show that God is pleased by the man who swears to his own hurt, and changes not; next, that when people have taken a lawful covenant upon them and broken it, "God will appear eminently in sending plagues upon them". Several Scripture passages are cited to prove this: Joshua 9, 2 Samuel 21, Jeremiah 34, and the text of the sermon. Then he speaks against the idea that a Pope can dissolve the obligation of a covenant, oath or treaty, and then proceeds to "uses", of which he lists three, the sum of which is that covenant breaking is sin and will be punished by God. Finally, he takes up "some things which folk may have for excusing themselves about the Solemn League and Covenant; and for understanding of them, consider, the Parliament of Scotland, England, and Ireland, entered into a covenant for maintaining the word of God and the purity thereof, and putting away profanity; and engaged themselves against schism, heresy, error, Popery and Prelacy. And there was an oath of God taken for this end upon us, and our King took it at his coronation. This oath again is broken by our King and Parliament, and is despised, for which, according to the word of God, wrath will be upon the heads of those that have broken it, if God do not mercifully prevent it". "Now, there are many that have many excuses and many objections about this Solemn League and Covenant. I shall, therefore, speak to some of them, and I take you to record this day, I pretend not to preach rebellion against King or Parliament, but according to the word of God; and if it be rebellion, we must take our hazard of it". Following this eleven objections against the Solemn League and Covenant are taken up and answered one by one, as follows:

1. We are not bound by an oath or covenant which is not lawful but the Solemn League and Covenant was unlawful, because it lacked the consent of the King, i.e., since it was made by the Parliaments; Numbers 30:3-5 proves that the King could disallow the Covenant. Guthrie replies, that the King is a civil parent, not a natural one, and therefore the text is irrelevant; Numbers 30:2 shows that a man's vows or a widow's must stand, being once made; God makes no exception but that of a woman in her father's house or subject to her husband; this is the only exception allowed by Scripture, therefore the Covenant must stand; even if the King did not take the Covenant when it was made, the authority of Parliament was sufficient to make it lawful. The King afterwards subscribed the Covenant, therefore it must stand.

2. The King did take the Covenant, it is admitted, but he may break it, because he took it not freely, but was forced to do so. To this Guthrie replies, that no one would have ventured at the time to say that the King was forced to it. But even if he was forced to take it, it is still binding; even though the act was not spontaneous, it was none the less voluntary. Zedekiah was a captive of the king of Babylon, and so was forced to make a covenant with the king of Babylon; when later he broke the oath, God's vengeance came upon him for it.

3. The Solemn League and Covenant must be broken, because we are not bound to keep with them that broke to us first; but England first broke the Covenant, therefore Scotland is released from the bond. Guthrie replies that those who make this objection must have never read the Covenant itself. It is not a bargain between three parties on earth, the one whereof breaking, the other is free. "But these three lands are one party, and the God of heaven is the other party; therefore, though England should break, should Scotland also break the Covenant? It is not after this tenor:-We will endeavour reformation in these lands, but if you break, we will break also. No; it is each man swearing for himself that he shall, in his place and station, endeavour reformation, so that if it were all left to one man, he must endeavour reformation. For, consider the last words of the article. Each of them for himself did lift up his hands to the Most High; and so these three lands are one party, and the other party is the God of heaven...".

4. "We swear in the League and Covenant to that which is impossible, and therefore it cannot be kept". Guthrie replies that this objection assumes that Scotland is sworn to reform England, or that England is sworn to reform Scotland,

which is impossible, etc. But this is not the obligation of the Covenant. It does not bind the swearers to *accomplish* the reformation of England, "but that which is sworn is this: they are each to endeavour in their places and callings, the reformation of religion in doctrine, worship, discipline, and government in these lands, and to reform England, according to the word of God, and the best reformed Churches". This would have been a binding obligation even if no covenant had been sworn; the objection proceeds not from principle but from malice against the word of God. "If the king and parliament were studying to reform, as much as they are studying to deface and deform, there should be no need of this objection".

5. The Covenant was too rashly entered into, and therefore is not binding. To this Guthrie gives three replies. First, it was not indeliberate, but the result of a long development. Second, it was deliberated more than many oaths in Scripture, which are acknowledged by all parties to have been binding. Third, even Joshua's covenant with the Gibeonites was binding and could not be broken, though rashly entered into without taking counsel with the Lord; the Solemn League and Covenant was entered into after much seeking of the Lord's mind, therefore is still more binding.

6. "The Covenant cannot be binding, because the parties dealt craftily with us". Guthrie replies: first, England is not the party covenanted with; the three lands together are the one party, and God the other party with whom they covenanted; second, Joshua chapter 9 shows this objection to be without weight; the Gibeonites used craft, and seduced Joshua and the princes, yet the covenant was binding.

7. The terms of the Covenant are so general that it cannot be regarded as binding; it is an oath to endeavour the

reformation of England according to the best reformed Churches, but these are not specified by name, therefore it cannot stand. Guthrie replies, first, that if any one wants a more particular rule than the word of God for reformation, he must go to another land to seek another Gospel from Jews or Turks; and if so, then Scotland has no standard at all. Second, by comparing one part of the Covenant with another, the matter becomes quite plain. The reformation proposed must not be Popery, nor Prelacy, for these are rejected by it; this leaves only Independency and Presbytery, "and, at that time, Independency was to be brought to Presbytery," therefore it was to be a Presbyterian reformation.

8. "Supposing the Covenant binds the land, yet it binds none but those that took it". To this objection Guthrie replies: "Now I perceive there are many of you young and ranting blades, that think yourselves happy youths because ye never took the covenant. But I have a word to speak to such from the Scriptures, and therefore take it with you: Wherever a king and the princes of land take a covenant the rest of the land are bound to it, as you may see in that covenant with the Gibeonites. The people there did not swear, yea, they murmured against the oath; but though the people did not swear, yet the princes say, 'We have sworn unto the Lord, we cannot touch them'. Therefore do not beguile yourselves. Ye stand as surely engaged to it as I or he who did subscribe it with our hands, therefore the breach of it shall be required at your hands, be you young or old, men or women; and remember 'The children of Israel did not smite them, because the princes had sworn the oath'.   Might not the people have said, 'let them keep it, who did swear it'? But it is not so; for they say, 'We have all sworn it, therefore we must not touch them' ".

9. "Suppose it binds this generation, yet it cannot

bind our posterity". Guthrie answers: "This same generation that did swear it hath broken it, and I fear the same generation shall be punished for it. The covenant did directly bind all following generations,-- 'that our children after us be found walking in faith and love, that the Lord may dwell among us'. These are the very words of the covenant. For what end were these words put in? Was it not to bind our posterity, and to keep uniformity and unity, and to bind them to the word of God? But you will say, 'There is no mention of the posterity'. There was no mention made of the posterity of Israel, when the people of Israel made that covenant with the Gibeonites, neither was there mention made of the Gibeonites' posterity; yet you may see the covenant binding on their posterity (Josh. ix.; 2 Sam. xxi.). So, then, you must understand that the covenant is absolute; therefore I conclude, that as sure as sun and moon endure in the firmament, if there be any generation in these three lands, God will require the breach of His covenant at their hands, and His vengeance shall be upon them, if they repent not".

10. "The King and Estates of the land found hurt in keeping it". Guthrie answers: "Ay, but 'He that sweareth to his own hurt and changeth not' ".

11. "There will be eminent advantages by the breaking of it, *ergo* ". Guthrie replies: there could be no advantage to the three lands comparable to the advantage of the Solemn League. There would have been eminent advantages in breaking the covenant with the Gibeonites, but God did not allow the people to do so. So in the case of Zedekiah's covenant with the king of Babylon; it was all to his advantage to break it, but it was wrong.

Having answered these eleven objections to the binding obligation of the Covenant, Guthrie proceeds to show that those who break the Covenant will suffer judgment for it. He warns against partaking of other men's sins, lest we partake of their plagues "Suppose there were but one family in these lands that would stand to it, and if all that family should turn their back upon it except one person, truly that person is bound to stand to it". Finally he protests that he is not preaching treason: "This is no rebellion or treason, and those who think it censurable I commit to the prophets who are gone to their place, who did these things. First punish them, and then me. I commit all these things unto you. The Lord engrave them on your hearts! Amen". [19]

The foregoing is probably fairly representative of the arguments used by the Covenanters in the persecuting and post-Revolution periods to prove the continuing obligation of the Scottish Covenants. In essence it is an argument that the Covenants were (1) moral in character; (2) Scriptural in content; (3) taken by the lawful rulers and representatives of the nation; (4) purported to be, and were in their nature, perpetual bonds; and therefore (5) are perpetually binding on the Church and nation of Scotland.

Patrick Walker left the United Societies after the Revolution, but continued to maintain the perpetual obligation of the Covenants. It was a great grief to him that these were not recognized by the Revolution Church. He writes that "the General Assembly, and Commissioners at London, in the year 1644, Henderson, Gillespie, and Rutherfoord, and their brethren the English divines, called the Solemn League and Covenant the foundation and chief part of their work, and obligation of it perpetual that no power on earth could loose. It must be a strange building that we have now, that wants both foundation and chief part; but they are now upon another

---

[19] Howie, John (ed.),*Sermons Delivered in Times Of Persecution in Scotland, by Sufferers for the Royal Prerogatives of Jesus Christ,* pp. 661-674.

footing".[20]   After the Revolution a sect arose in Scotland which not merely ignored the Covenants, as did the Revolution Church, but preached that they were actually unscriptural and immoral bonds. This was the sect of the Glassites, followers of a Mr. Glass or Glas. They affirmed that national covenanting was an institution peculiar to the Jews.[21]   Walker writes of them thus: "Mr. Glass striking at the foundation of our Covenanted Reformation, overturning the constitution, government and discipline of this Church, which was never heard of before in Scotland". He continues, that this was a breach of ordination vows, that Glass denied the lawfulness of national covenanting under the New Testament dispensation, and held that all the martyrs who had died adhering to the Covenants had died so far unenlightened.[22]

5.   The Perpetual Obligation of the Covenants the Formal Principle of the Covenanting Movement.

There is every reason to believe that in 1638 and 1643 the subscribers of the National Covenant and the Solemn League and Covenant universally believed these bonds to be of perpetual obligation. Through the twenty-eight years of persecution which followed the Restoration in 1660 this principle was unlawful in the Church and nation of Scotland, but was maintained by the Covenanters who dissented from the Prelatic Church and maintained separate ordinances in the form of conventicles. As the number of one-time Covenanters who conformed to the Prelatic Church increased, the number of dissenters who maintained the principle of the continuing obligation of the Covenants decreased proportionately. This

---

[20] Walker, Patrick, *Six Saints of the Covenant*, I, p. 11.

[21] *Ibid.*, I, p. 278.

[22] *Ibid.*, I, pp. 150-151.

principle was ignored in the Revolution Settlement, although there was some sentiment in the Revolution Church in favor of the National Covenant (but not the Solemn League and Covenant).[23] In the period immediately after the Revolution Settlement, the principle of the perpetual obligation of the Covenants was publicly maintained only by the United Societies and by some very small fragmentary dissenting sects, to which reference has been made in Part II.[24]

The principle of the perpetual obligation of the Covenants was the formal principle of the Covenanting Movement in the sense that this principle was characteristic of Covenanters as such in distinction from Presbyterians as such. Every Covenanter was a Presbyterian but not every Presbyterian was a Covenanter. Those who held the principle of the perpetual obligation of the Covenants were Covenanters, both before and after the Revolution Settlement. And it was this principle that determined the nature of the other distinctive principles held by the United Societies and the Reformed Presbyterian Church. Because they believed in the perpetual obligation of the Covenants, they believed that the Church and nation of Scotland were sworn and bound to maintain the sole headship of Christ over the Church, and a Christian form of civil constitution.

The principle of the perpetual obligation of the Covenants, however, has not been maintained solely by the Reformed Presbyterian Church. It was also maintained by the Associate or Secession Church, although the inferences drawn from it were different from those drawn by the Reformed Presbyterians. The Judicial Testimony of the Associate Presbytery (1737) provided as a query to be answered by

---

[23] Hutchison, Matthew, *The Reformed Presbyterian Church in Scotland. Its Origin and History, 1680-1876*, p. 141.

[24] Supra, pp. 162-165.

candidates for licensure the following: "Do you own the
binding obligation of the National Covenant, particularly as
explained in 1638, to abjure Prelacy and the five articles of
Perth; and of the Solemn League of the three kingdoms,
particularly as renewed in Scotland in 1648, with an
acknowledgment of sins; and will you study to prosecute the
ends thereof"?[25]   The Judicial Testimony affirmed the
perpetual obligation of the Covenants in the following words:
"In like manner they do hereby own and assert the perpetual
obligation of the National Covenant of Scotland, frequently
subscribed by persons of all ranks in this kingdom... as also
they own and assert the perpetual obligation of the Solemn
League and Covenant ... Likewise they hereby declare their
adherence to the several Testimonies, Declarations and
Warnings emitted in behalf of the Covenanted Reformation of
this Church from the year 1650 to the year 1688; particularly
to the contendings and wrestlings during that period,
whereby a great cloud of witnesses resisted unto blood in
testifying for the supremacy and headship of the Lord Jesus
over his own House, and other branches of our Covenanted
Reformation in opposition to abjured Prelacy".[26] In 1743 the
Associate Presbytery renewed the bond of the National
Covenant and the Solemn League and Covenant, with
religious services, and made approval of this deed a term of
ministerial and Christian communion.[27] The way in which the
Covenants were renewed was not satisfactory to the Rev.
Thomas Nairne, who left the Associate Church and joined the
Cameronians, enabling the Reformed Presbytery to be
constituted in 1743.[28] In the "bond" sworn by the Associate
Presbytery, the Covenants are merely mentioned as binding
the swearers to live together in the fear of God and their love

[25] Johnston, *op. cit*, pp. 171-172.

[26] *Ibid.*, pp. 172-173.

[27] *Ibid.*

[28] *Ibid.*, p. 174.

one to another.[29]

The principle of the perpetual obligation of the Covenants is maintained by two denominations in Scotland today, the Reformed Presbyterian Church and the United Original Secession Church. The Testimony of the latter Church states "that Covenants entered into by a people with God which are at once lawful and laudable in their matter and permanent in their objects lay the societies, civil or ecclesiastical, who enter into these Bonds, under continued obligation to discharge the duties engaged in from generation to generation. That, in accordance with this principle, they hold that the National Covenant of Scotland and the Solemn League and Covenant are, in so far as their objects or ends have not yet been gained, binding on us as they were binding on our fathers who entered into them; that the obligation descends in the same manner as the National Debt contracted by our forefathers falls to be paid by us. In short, the United Original Secession Church claims to be regarded as a branch of the Reformed and Covenanted Church of Scotland, witnessing in a state of secession for her Reformation principles...and...lifting up the banner of a judicial testimony on behalf of the perpetual and continued obligation of the National, and of the Solemn League and Covenant...".[30] Strictly, then, the Cameronians or Reformed Presbyterians are not the only body in Scotland entitled to be called "Covenanters" today, for this name must be shared with the United Original Secession Church. Likewise, the principle of the perpetual obligation of the covenants is not, strictly speaking, a distinctive principle of the Reformed Presbyterian Church, for it is also held by the United Original Secession Church. But since the Cameronians or United Societies were the only body publicly maintaining this principle from 1690

---

[29] *Ibid.*, pp. 174-176.

[30] *Ibid.*, p. 177.

to 1733, the present study regards the term "Covenanter" as practically equivalent to "Cameronian" and "Reformed Presbyterian".

The Covenants were publicly renewed by the Reformed Presbyterians at Crawfordjohn in 1745, concerning which the Historical Testimony of the Reformed Presbyterian Church of Scotland speaks as follows: "this was the last instance in which the public Covenants were renewed in the Reformed Presbyterian Church, we beg here to offer the following observations: — 1st. That covenanting is an occasional duty, to be performed as the circumstances of the Church or of a nation may seem to demand; and that the permanent obligation of the Covenants of these lands depends on their moral and scriptural character, rather than on their being publicly recognized or renewed. 2nd. Yet we believe, that where a Church or people have been brought under the bond of such engagements, it is a duty warranted by reason and Scripture occasionally to renew them, as the aspects of Divine Providence may require. 3rd. We believe that the defection of a great majority of a Church or nation from such Covenants does not cancel their obligation; and that the call upon a minority, who adheres to them, to bring them up to remembrance, becomes the more urgent when the public acts of the majority have a tendency to bury them in oblivion. 4th. We approve of the zeal and faithfulness which prompted our fathers to engage in this work at seasonable times, and admit that we are placed under super-added obligations to adhere to these Covenants in consequence of their deeds of renovation".[31] This represents the position of the Reformed Presbyterian Church of Scotland on this principle at the present day.

---

[31] *Ibid.*, pp. 454-455, referring to *Historical Testimony of the Reformed Presbyterian Church of Scotland*, p. 187.

CHAPTER II

THE SOLE HEADSHIP OF CHRIST
OVER THE CHURCH

1.   **The Anti-Erastian Character of the
      Covenanter Movement.**

A. P. Stanley, an Anglican writer, speaks of "that extreme sensitiveness of the Scottish clergy to regal or legislative interference, which Hallam well calls 'Presbyterian Hildebrandism', which has caused the name 'Erastian' to be placed in the blackest list of heresies".[1] This sensitiveness is the result of long contending for a principle which was characteristic of the Covenanting movement, the principle of the sole headship of Jesus Christ over His House, the Church. While some of the Reformed Churches on the Continent saw no harm in an Erastian establishment of religion, and while the Church of England, since the Reformation, has always been an Erastian establishment, this idea early became anathema in Scotland. The fact is that unlike most other Protestant countries, Scotland was not reformed by the civil magistrate from above, but by popular religious teachers who permeated the whole of society with their doctrines. The General Assembly of the Church of Scotland which came into being in 1560 was not the creature of the State nor was it subject to the civil magistrate at that time.

The opposition to Erastianism in Scotland can be traced to a very early period. In 1561 John Knox said to

[1] Stanley, Arthur Penrhyn, *Lectures on the History of the Church of Scotland, Delivered in Edinburgh in 1872*, p. 79; the quotation is from Hallam, *Constitutional History of England*, III, p. 421.

Maitland of Lethington, who had challenged the right of the General Assembly to meet without the Queen's consent, "Take from us the liberty of assemblies, and take from us the gospel. If the liberty of the Church must depend upon her allowance or disallowance, we shall want not only assemblies, but the preaching of the gospel".[2]

Much of the history of the Church of Scotland after the time of Knox has been the history of a desperate struggle to maintain the spiritual independence of the Church, the principle of the sole headship of Christ over the Church, in the face of Erastian encroachments on the part of the civil power. These encroachments became most severe during the period of persecution between the Restoration and the Revolution, but were also characteristic of a large part of the period before the Second Reformation and of the period after the Revolution Settlement.

The Church of the Second Reformation, which the later Covenanters always regarded as the purest period of the Church of Scotland, was not Erastian in character, notwithstanding allegations that have been made by some writers that it was.[3] It is true that the Confession of Faith and other standards were ratified by acts of Parliament, but this did not constitute Erastianism, for the Parliament merely stated its formal approbation of what had already been authoritatively determined by the General Assembly. Nor did it violate the principle of the sole headship of Christ over the Church, for the position of the Second Reformation was precisely that Christ was the Head of the State as well as of the Church. The land, as well as the Church, had been given away in Covenant to be the Lord's. The Covenants had been accepted by Parliament, as well as by the General Assembly.

---

[2] Hetherington, W. M., *History of the Church of Scotland*, p. 100.

[3] Stanley, *op. cit.*, pp. 77-78.

They were civil, as well as ecclesiastical bonds. They bound the nation as such, as well as the Church. So for the Christian State to sanction what had been done by the Christian Church did not usurp any of Christ's prerogatives, for Christ was the Head of both   Church and State. Erastianism is not *any* connection of the State with the Church or with religion, but *the claim of the State to be supreme over the Church* , so that the Church is not a coordinate authority with the State but an inferior authority under the State. The civil and ecclesiastical constitution of Scotland at the Second Reformation was one which provided for a union of Church and State, but that union was not of an Erastian character.

The Covenanters' opposition to Erastianism was manifested in many situations after the Second Reformation. They protested against the dissolution of the General Assembly by Cromwell's forces in 1653. They opposed the legislation which made the King supreme in causes ecclesiastical after the Restoration. They opposed the Indulgences, because these flowed from that usurped supremacy in causes ecclesiastical. And finally they opposed the Revolution Settlement because of the Erastian method by which it was brought about, the lead being taken throughout by the civil magistrate, and because of the Erastian character of the Settlement itself, the Church being dependent on the civil magistrate for the summoning and dissolving of its supreme judicatory.   The Covenanters were often regarded as unyielding, extreme and even fanatical, but they were contending for a principle, and when men are contending for a principle, obstinacy is a virtue. The man who can yield the smallest fraction of an inch of ground on a real and valid principle is at heart a compromiser, and when times become difficult, he will usually be found "at ease in Zion" or walking indifferently down the middle of the road maintaining what the Covenanters called a "detestable neutrality".

2.   The Covenanters Not Opposed to the Principle of Establishment.

The fact that the Covenanters always opposed Erastianism, and scorned all compromise of the principle of Christ's sole headship over the Church, does not mean that they were opposed to the idea of an established or national Church, or that they believed in the separation of Church and State as it is commonly understood in America today. A reading of the Solemn League and Covenant is sufficient to show that that document is based upon the philosophy of Christian civil government and presupposes the idea of an established Church. The modern idea that the State has nothing to do with religion and the Church nothing to do with politics, the Covenanters would have utterly abhorred and anathematized.

The conception of the relation between the Church and State held by the Covenanters was, in brief, that both are divine institutions, each independent and supreme in its own sphere, united in an alliance of mutual support and helpfulness, the Church to teach the Christian doctrine of the civil magistrate, and the State to establish the Church by appropriate legislation and to provide for its financial support out of the national resources. According to this view, the fact that the Church is established by the State as the national Church, does not imply that the State has the right to dictate the policy or review the decisions of the Church. The Church is subject only to Christ, though by law established as the national Church.

---

[4] Hewison, James King, *The Covenanters: A History of the Church in Scotland From the Reformation to the Revolution*, I, p. 85.

This view of the relation between the Church and the State has its roots in the Second Book of Discipline (1578), where it is set forth in considerable detail. According to the Second Book of Discipline, the "power and policy" of the Church "is different and distinct in the own nature from that power and policy which is called the civil power, and appertains to the civil government of the commonwealth, albeit they be both of God, and tend to one end, that is, to advance the glory of God, and to have godly and good subjects".[5] "Notwithstanding as the ministers and others of the ecclesiastical state are subject to the magistrate civilly, so ought the person of the magistrate to be subject to the Church spiritually and in ecclesiastical government".[6] "The civil power should command the spiritual to exercise and to do their office according to the word of God; the spiritual rulers should require the Christian magistrate to minister justice and punish vice, and to maintain the liberty of the Church, and quietness within their bounds".[7] "The magistrate ought neither preach, minister the sacraments, nor execute the censures of the Church, nor yet prescribe any rule how it should be done, but command the minister to observe the rule prescribed in the word, and punish transgressors by civil means; the minister again exercises not the civil jurisdiction, but teaches the magistrate how it should be exercised according to the word".[8] "The magistrate ought to assist, maintain, and fortify this jurisdiction of the Church; the ministers should assist their princes in all things agreeable to the word, providing they neglect not their charge in involving

---

[5] Spottiswoode, John, *History of the Church of Scotland*, 203-1625, II, p. 233, quoting the *Second Book of Discipline*, I, 8.

[6] *Ibid.*, II, p. 234; *Second Book of Discipline*, I. 13.

[7] *Ibid.*, II. p. 234; *Second Book of Discipline*, I. 16.

[8] *Ibid.*, II, p. 235; *Second Book of Discipline*, I. 20.

themselves in civil affairs".[9] "Although all members of the Church are holden, according to their vocation, to advance the kingdom of Christ Jesus so far as lies in their power; yet chiefly Christian princes, kings and other magistrates are holden to do the same, for they are called in the Scripture nurses of the Church, because by them it is, or at least ought to be, maintained and defended against all those that would procure the hurt thereof".[10] The principles thus laid down in the Second Book of Discipline represent substantially, though not always precisely, the ground taken on the relation of Church and State by the Covenanters and Reformed Presbyterians through their history to the present day.

3.   The Effectiveness of the Covenanters' Testimony for the Sole Headship of Christ over the Church.

Of the three distinctive doctrines of the Covenanters, the principle of the sole headship of Christ over the Church is the only one that has been at all widely accepted outside of Cameronian and Reformed Presbyterian circles. Their testimony for this principle was a major reason, perhaps the supreme reason, for their refusal to incorporate with the Church of the Revolution Settlement in 1690. They were the only body that publicly protested against the Erastianism of the Revolution Settlement *at the time* . The later history of the Revolution Church, and especially the patronage controversy and the Secession and Relief movements and the Disruption of 1843 have shown that the Covenanters were correct in alleging that the Revolution Settlement was Erastian in nature and that the Revolution Church was in bondage to the State. These movements of secession were not protests against the pure principle of Erastianism, however, so much as protests

---

[9] *Ibid.*, II, p. 235; *Second Book of Discipline*, I. 21.

[10] *Ibid.* II, p. 247; *Second Book of Discipline*, X. 1.

against practices which resulted from the Erastian establishment of the Church. The Covenanters objected not merely to the abuses and practical evils when these occurred, but to the *principle of Erastianism* in the Revolution Church, prior to and apart from all actual working out of this principle in specific overt acts of dominion of the State over the Church. Even if the Revolution State had set a record of model conduct in relation to the Revolution Church, and even if the patronage controversy had never taken place, the Covenanters would have been opposed to the principle of Erastianism which they saw in the constitution of the Revolution Church.

The various secessions from the Revolution Church were, however, protests against Erastianism, either in practice, or in theory and practice both, and in this respect they no doubt were to a considerable extent fruits of the publicly expressed dissent of the Covenanters from the Revolution Settlement. The uniqueness of the Covenanters' testimony consists in the fact that they were the first to maintain this principle after the Revolution Settlement, and the only ones to maintain it at the time of that Settlement. What they alone maintained at that time became wide-spread in later times. It is needless to add that the principle of the sole headship of Christ over the Church is today maintained by Presbyterian and other bodies in many countries where the separation of Church and State, in the modern sense, is the rule. The separation of Church and State as ordinarily understood today, however, never was a doctrine of Covenanters or Reformed Presbyterians in Scotland.

CHAPTER III

THE COVENANTERS' DOCTRINE OF CHRISTIAN CIVIL GOVERNMENT

1. The Mediatorial Kingship of Christ over the Nations.

The Reformed Presbyterian doctrine concerning the kingship of Christ over the nations is that Christ, not merely in his divine nature, as God, but in his mediatorial capacity, as God-man, has been appointed by God the Father to rule over the nations, and indeed over the universe, during the present age and until the end of the world. Reformed Presbyterians reject as erroneous the doctrines "that Christ's mediatorial power is restricted to saints or to His church",[1] "that civil rulers are not, in their official character, subject to the Messiah and bound to recognize His revealed will and promote the interests of His kingdom",[2] and "that nations and associations of men are not, in their corporate capacity, subject to the law and authority of Christ".[3] They hold that Christ "has authority over nations, governors, and legislatures, and it is their duty to own and obey Him".[4]

This doctrine of the mediatorial kingship of Christ over the nations as such does not appear to be traceable farther back than the period of the Second Reformation.

[1] *Testimony of the Reformed Presbyterian Church of Ireland* , Part I (Doctrinal and Practical), p. 38.

[2] *Ibid.*

[3] *Ibid.*

[4] *Summary of the Testimony of the Reformed Presbyterian Church of Scotland*, p. 46.

Before that there had been a clear conception of civil government as a divine institution, of the relation between Church and State, and of the lawfulness of resisting and even of punishing tyrants.[5] But in the period of the Second Reformation the idea was held that the nation as such had, by its Covenant, accepted Christ as King, not only of the Church, but of the commonwealth as well. One of Rutherford's letters exemplifies this conception: "Alas! that we will not pull and draw Him to his old tents again, to come and feed among the lilies till the day breaks and the shadows flee away. O, that the nobles would come, in the strength and courage of the Lord, to bring our lawful King Jesus here again. I am persuaded that He shall return in glory to this land; but happy sure they who would help convey Him to this country, and set Him up again on the mercy-seat between the cherubim. O Sun, return again to darkened Britain!...I know He can also triumph in suffering, and weep, and reign, and die, and triumph, and remain in prison, and yet subdue his enemies. But how happy could I live to see the Coronation-day of Christ, to see his mother who bare Him put the crown upon His head again, and cry with shouting, till the earth shall sing, 'Lord Jesus, our King, live and reign for evermore' ".[6] To be sure this might be understood to refer only to Christ's headship over the Church, but the probability is that it included the nation as well.

During the period of persecution the doctrine of Christ's kingship over the nation became more clearly defined. There are a number of references to this doctrine in

---

[5] Buchanan, George, *De Jure Regni apud Scotos, or Dialogue Concerning the True Privilege of Government in the Kingdom of Scotland,* described in Johnston, John C., *Treasury of the Scottish Covenant,* p. 258; *Second Book of Discipline* (1578); John Knox, *letter to the Scottish nobles on resistance to supreme rulers, written from Dieppe, 1557.*

[6] Stanley, Arthur Penrhyn, *Lectures on the History of the Church of Scotland, Delivered in Edinburgh in 1872,* p. 106.

the sermons of Richard Cameron. Cameron conceived of the doctrine of Christ's kingship as implying that there could be no lawful magistrate except in subjection to Christ: "There is none to help you at all, except you acknowledge Him as your King and head, and except you acknowledge no other magistrate but according to what He ordains in His word",[7] Preaching in 1680 on Hosea 13:9-10, he said, "Our Lord is saying, 'I will tell you what are the terms; if you would have help from Me you must take Me to be your King; you must take Me to be the Head of the Church'. Our Lord Jesus is and must be King upon His holy hill of Zion. There is no king in the Church besides Him".... " 'I will be thy king' supposes more than this: ye shall have no other king besides Me. I will tell you, the most part of the land cry out, We will have no other king but Caesar—no other king but king Charles. But we must cry we will have no other king but Christ. What is that, Say ye, Are ye against all monarchy and civil Government, We are much taken up with that, if God let pure government be established, that is most for the good and advantage of civil and ecclesiastical society. But we set up kings and princes, but not by Him. If ye would have Him be for you ye must cut off this king, and these princes, and make able men be your rulers, endued with suitable qualifications both of body and mind, that may employ their power for the cause and interest of God. What would we do with such persons as state themselves in opposition to God? If we had the zeal of God within us we would not call him our king, and even with regard to the nobles and magistrates of this land we would not acknowledge them to be magistrates"..."Our Lord will set up other magistrates according to His promise: 'And kings shall be thy nursing fathers, and queens thy nursing mothers'. And who knows but God will make out that yet? 'And their nobles shall be of

---

[7] Howie, John (ed.), *Sermons Delivered in Times of Persecution in Scotland, by Sufferers for the Royal Prerogatives of Jesus Christ*, p. 417.

themselves, and their governor shall proceed from the midst of them'. Indeed by governor we principally understand our Lord Jesus Christ. But when He turns back the captivity of His Church and people, none shall be governors but such as shall be for Him, at least by profession. Indeed when our king was set up in better case than we are now in, he professed himself to be a Presbyterian, though any rational man might have known he was but a treacherous man. It was but a dreadful mocking of God to require such oaths of him who would be bound by no oath. Yea, none of them will be bound by any oath whatever. And now are ye ready to take Christ for your king in the sense we have explained".[8] Preaching on Isaiah 49:24-26, Cameron said: "I do not desire to reflect upon our fathers for bringing home Charles Stuart to get the crown; ...yea, his actions since, and the connivances of those who had his favour or any power under him, evidence that it is impossible to manifest or maintain the royal prerogatives of Jesus Christ and yet maintain the king's civil rights. Since it is so declared that we must either quit him as king or Christ, indeed for my part I am for no king but Jesus Christ, since they will have none but Caesar. When Christ is seated upon His throne and His crown upon His head, let such magistrates be appointed in every particular station as will employ their power for the advancement of His kingdom, and for destroying the kingdom of darkness in this land and in every place where Christ shall reign; and then let them be owned".[9]

Alexander Shields, preaching at the end of the period of persecution (March 11th, 1688) stated that the Covenanters' disowning the king and magistrates was no new doctrine but a principle long recognized in Scotland: "Was not Charles I. opposed by two armies, and his son

---

[8] *Ibid.*, pp. 413 ff.

[9] *Ibid.*, p 450.

Charles II. refused to be admitted to the government till he subscribed the covenants? Did not our Church, by their acts and constitutions, declare what magistrates they would have reign over them, and what qualifications were requisite to them? So that what we have done in disowning the present authority is no new nice notion, but consonant to the principles of the Church of Scotland. It is those that own the authority of the Popish usurper that espouse new notions and not we: for this principle is maintained by the generality of the enemies thereof, that when by providence any are in government, they have a right to govern. This is to make the Holy One the author of sin (seeing that though the ordinance and office of magistracy be according to His preceptive and approbative will), yet tyranny cannot be, but only by His permission and providential will; for where tyranny is, it is the throne of iniquity, which is the throne of the devil, which should not be owned".[10]

It will be seen from the foregoing that during the period of persecution the Covenanters drew a distinction between the preceptive will of God and the providential will of God. Tyranny might exist by the providential will of God, but it could not exist by the preceptive will of God. It might be God's providential ordinance, but it could not be God's moral ordinance, for that would be to make God the author of sin. For God to command approval of magistrates which were not his moral ordinance, would be for God to command approval of that which God himself did not approve, which could not be. The Covenanters, therefore, disowned the civil magistrate as contrary to the revealed will of God and the kingship of Christ over the nation.

The whole testimony of the Covenanters on this subject must be understood in the light of the Covenants.

---

[10] *Ibid.*, pp. 596-597.

Scotland was not simply a kingdom; it was a kingdom that had been given away to be the Lord's by solemn Covenant, and that Covenant had been sworn by the civil power as well as by the Church. The situation in which they were placed after the Restoration was not simply that of Christians living under a non-Christian form of civil government, but Christians living in a land which had by covenant recognized the kingship of Christ over the nation and which had later by legislative act repudiated that Covenant. The Stuart government was not simply a non-Christian government; it was a perjured usurpation of Christ's crown already placed on his head in Scotland. The Covenanters therfore not merely dissented from the civil constitution but declared the whole system in its entirety to be positively unlawful and the magistrates to be no magistrates. Since the Covenants were ignored in the Revolution Settlement, they continued this attitude of protest in the post-Revolution period. In 1693 four persons who had been imprisoned before the Revolution were liberated from prison. Together they signed a protest stating that they had been detained a long time by "the present pretended powers" and that hearing of their designed liberation, they wished the world to know that they were not liberated because of any petition made to the government whom they "could neither own nor supplicate as our lawfull rullers".[11]

In more modern times the Reformed Presbyterians have considerably modified the position taken during the persecuting period and at the Revolution Settlement, by the introduction of two distinctions. The first of these is the distinction between countries favored with the light of divine revelation and lands not so favored. "In every nation which professes Christianity it is the duty of civil rulers, including

---

[11] Walker, Patrick, *Six Saints of the Covenant*, II, p. 233 quoting Laing MSS, Vol. 344, No. 300.

not only kings, presidents, ministers of State, legislators and magistrates, but also political electors, to honour the King of Kings and Lord of Lords by moulding the national life and laws according to the principles laid down in Scripture for nations".[12] "If a nation that is favoured with the light of divine revelation rejects in its constitution and legislation the heavenly light thus bestowed; still more, if a nation that has pledged itself by covenant to be the Lord's, or otherwise made high attainments in that recognition of Christ and His will, turns away from Him again and renounces its obligation and allegiance; the Christian, to be faithful to his Lord, must dissent and separate himself from the nation, because of its rebellion against Christ".[13] On the other hand, the Christian who lives in a land not illuminated with the light of Scripture "may even co-operate with and befriend the government, if he be allowed to act according to the law of God and the dictates of an enlightened conscience and without coming under any unchristian obligation".[14]

The second distinction is the distinction between *obeying* a government which rejects Christ, and *incorporating* with such a government. Even under a covenant-breaking and Christ-rejecting civil government, the Christian ought to be subject to the government and obey the laws in all things not contrary to the law of God. He ought to submit to every ordinance of man for the Lord's sake. "It is the duty of Christians to give their support to whatever is in itself moral, praiseworthy, and beneficent, in the administration under which they live, and as much as in them lies to be quiet and peaceable in their deportment, and thus to promote the peace

---

[12] *Summary of the Testimony of the Reformed Presbyterian Church of Scotland*, p. 56.

[13] *Testimony of the Reformed Presbyterian Church of Ireland*, Part I (Doctrinal and Practical), p. 110.

[14] *Ibid.*, p.111.

and order of society and other ends of good government.
When the government, though antichristian, grants civil and
religious liberty, Christians may, quite consistently with their
testimony, pay their share of the common taxation in return
for the protection and other advantages which they receive;
but they may not pay taxes levied for an immoral purpose or
exacted as a pledge of allegiance to an unscriptural
constitution".[15] Even though the government is not regarded
as God's moral ordinance, it is God's providential ordinance
and the Christian should be subject to it in all things moral
and lawful.   But this is a very different thing from
incorporating with the civil government, which would in
effect amount not merely to submitting to the government but
actually becoming a part of the government itself, and which,
in a democracy, would take the form of holding public office
or exercising the elective franchise. There are two possible
relationships between the Christian citizen and the civil
government. The first is the relationship between the subject
and the ruler, or between the citizen and the civil magistrate,
which implies obedience and submission. This relationship is
legitimate in all things lawful, even when the civil
government is not definitely Christian in its constitution and
character. The other relationship is the relationship between
the Christian as a member of the political body and the civil
government. In this relationship the Christian is not ruled but
a ruler; he is not subject to the government, but a part of the
government; as an office-holder or voter he has incorporated
with the political society and is an integral part of the same.
The Reformed Presbyterian principle is, that this second
relationship ought to exist only when the civil government is
constituted on a definitely Christian basis. The first
relationship implies simply recognition of a fact, namely that
a certain civil government exists as the providential ordinance
of God, and that in this sense the powers that be are ordained

---

[15] *Ibid.*

of God, and ought to be obeyed by Christians except when they command something which is contrary to God's commandments; the first relationship implies, then, no *approval* of the government or its constitution, but simply the recognition that by God's permission it exists and therefore ought to be obeyed in things moral so long as it continues to exist. The second relationship, that of incorporation with the political body, implies approval of the constitution, for it makes the Christian an integral part of the government and therefore responsible for the character and policies of the same. This is the Reformed Presbyterian conception as it is held today in Scotland, Ireland and America; and it will be observed that this is a considerable modification of the doctrine as held, for example, at the time of the Revolution Settlement. Covenanters today hold that the civil constitution of Britain is defective, and that Christians, while they ought to obey the government in all things not contrary to God's commandments, yet ought not to incorporate with the .government, become a part of the governing body, swear allegiance to the constitution or express approval of the constitution so long as the constitution does not recognize Christ's kingship over the nation. The constitution is regarded as defective, and the magistrates as ruling upon a wrong basis, but still they are magistrates and to be obeyed in their legitimate commands. But at the Revolution the Covenanters positively disowned the government, and held that the magistrates were no magistrates, but "pretended magistrates". They appear to have confused two things which differ. One is the question of the right of the magistrate to rule; the other is the question of the duty of the Christian to obey the magistrate. Whether the magistrate has a moral right to rule is one question; according to the Covenanters, then and now, he has not, unless he recognizes the kingship of Christ and rules according to Scripture. Whether the Christian ought to obey even such magistrates as by divine providence are permitted to rule on a secular or non-Christian basis, is quite another question. The modern Reformed Presbyterian Testimonies recognize this elementary distinction, while the Covenanters at the time of the Revolution do not appear to have developed their conceptions to this point.

2. Scripture the Rule for the Regulation of Civil Affairs.

The Covenanters throughout the entire history of their movement have taken a very high view of Holy Scripture. They have held and hold today the plenary inspiration, entire sufficiency and supreme authority of the Scriptures of the Old and New Testaments, as set forth in the first chapter of the Westminster Confession of Faith. They regard the Bible not merely as the standard for religion and ecclesiastical matters in the strict sense, but as the supreme standard for all relationships and activities of life. Since the State is regarded as a divine institution, and the authority of the civil magistrate is derived from the kingly, office of Jesus Christ, it follows that the Word of God must be the standard for civil as well as for all other affairs. The civil magistrate must not be regarded as primarily the servant of society but as the minister of God to men for good. All legislation and administration should seek first the glory of God and second the benefit of society. Nations as such are bound to regulate their civil affairs by the moral law of God.[16] No sphere or department of human life can claim exemption from the authority of Scripture, and therefore in the sphere of civil government, rulers ought not merely to rule according to this standard, but ought to publicly profess to do so. The Bible should not only be the guide, but the officially recognized guide in civil affairs. This does not mean that the Bible is a text-book of political science or government, but that the principles revealed in Scripture must be applied to civil affairs as to all other affairs.

[16] *Ibid.*, p. 115.

This principle finds its expression, first of all, in the requirement that the nation as such recognize the mediatorial kingship of Christ and enter into covenant with Him. Second, it finds its expression in the requirement that holders of public office be possessed of Scriptural qualifications. The modern American idea that no religious test should be prescribed for public office is utterly contrary to the Covenanter position on civil government from the Second Reformation to the present day. The doctrine that public officials must be possessed of Scriptural qualifications is the basis of the Act of Classes which was passed in 1649. The same requirement found expression in the coronation oath which Charles II was required to take at Scone in 1651. The Queensferry Paper, Sanquhar Declaration and various later declarations, protests and testimonies set forth the same principle with more and more clearness and insistence. It was, however, no novelty, for it was the publicly approved and recognized position of the nation in 1649. The modern Reformed Presbyterian Testimonies do not approve of ecclesiastical or denominational tests for public office, but they do insist on the necessity of religious tests. For example the Irish Reformed Presbyterian Testimony rejects as an error the proposition "That atheists, agnostics, idolaters, deists, Arians, papists, pagans, political secularists, or any others who do not receive the Word of God as the supreme law for all relations of life, who do not profess the Christian faith, or whose lives are openly in conflict with Christian morality, may lawfully be civil rulers in a Christian nation".[17] This of course may be held to be an infringement on the rights of men, but it must be remembered that the whole emphasis of the Covenanter movement is on the rights of God, and that according to this viewpoint, men do not have any rights that conflict with the rights of God. Man cannot have any

---

[17] *Ibid.*

inalienable rights except those given by God himself; God gives to no man the right to be an unbeliever or to break the commandments; therefore no man has the right to these things; and the unbeliever, being in rebellion against God and Christ, has no right to hold office in a Christian nation which recognizes Christ as King and Scripture as its supreme standard. The Covenanter position is, in effect, a challenge of the modern secular state's *right to exist* in God's world. This position is held today by a very small number of people, but it is a position which can be traced back to the Scottish Church and nation of the Second Reformation.

3.   **The Uniqueness of the Reformed Presbyterian Doctrine of Christian Civil Government.**

The distinctive doctrines of the Covenanters have been enumerated as (1) the perpetual obligation of the Scottish Covenants; (2) the sole headship of Christ over the Church; and (3) Christian civil government. The first two of these are not really distinctive doctrines of Reformed Presbyterians today in the strict sense, for the first is also held by the United Original Secession Church, and the second has found general acceptance in many parts of the world, especially in countries where the Church and State are completely separated. There was a period, however (1661-1733) when these two doctrines were distinctive doctrines of the Covenanters, in the sense that they were the only body to give a public testimony for these doctrines during that period.

The third doctrine, the Reformed Presbyterian doctrine of Christian civil government, however, has been a distinctive doctrine of the Covenanters or Reformed Presbyterians ever since the overthrow of the Second Reformation, in the strict sense that no other Church or organization whatever has maintained a public profession of and witness for this doctrine. The various secessions from the Revolution Church in the eighteenth and nineteenth centuries were all protests against Erastianism in the relation between Church and State and against corruptions or abuses in the Church; none of them was a protest against the constitution of the State itself. This the Reformed Presbyterian position was and is, and it is this fact that sets the Reformed Presbyterian Church over against all other branches of the Presbyterian family in Scotland and in other countries. For this reason the Covenanter doctrine of Christian civil government, or of the mediatorial kingship of Christ over the nations, in the civil sphere, may justly be regarded as the material principle of the Covenanter movement from the Second Reformation to the present day.

A number of other principles are commonly spoken of as distinctive principles of the Reformed Presbyterian Church, but incorrectly so, for none of them is really distinctive, since all of them are held, to a greater or less extent, by other denominations at the present time. Historically speaking, the formal principle of the Covenanter movement is the perpetual obligation of the National Covenant and the Solemn League and Covenant, and the material principle is the mediatorial kingship of Christ over the nations. And as already stated, both of these principles and also the principle of the sole headship of Christ over the Church can be reduced to a single fundamental principle: *Ius Divinum* -divine right or the *rights of God* , which are to be recognized in the Church, the State and every sphere of life.

THE END.

BIBLIOGRAPHY

Act, Declaration, and Testimony, for the Whole of our Covenanted Reformation , (Ploughlandhead, Scotland, 1761); Philadelphia, 1876.

Cheetham, S., *A History of the Christian Church Since the Reformation* , 1907.

Cunningham, John, *The Church History of Scotland from the Commencement of the Christian Era to the Present Time* , 2 Vols., 1882.

Grub, George, *An Ecclesiastical History of Scotland from the Introduction of Christianity to the Present Time* . 4 Vols., 1861.

Henderson, Thomas (ed.), *Testimony Bearing Exemplified* , (Paisley, Scotland, 1791); New York, 1834; contains the *Informatory Vindication* .

Hetherington, W. M., *History of the Church of Scotland* , 1852.

Hewison, James King, *The Covenanters: A History of the Church of Scotland from the Reformation to the Revolution* . 2 Vols., 1908.

Horne, C. Silvester, *A Popular History of the Free Churches*, 1903.

Howie, John (ed.), *Sermons Delivered in Times of Persecution in Scotland, by Sufferers for the Royal Prerogatives of Jesus Christ* , 1880.

Howie, John, *The Scots Worthies* , 1781. (Some editions of this work are entitled Biographica Scoticana).

Hutchison, Matthew, *The Reformed Presbyterian Church in Scotland. Its Origin and History; 1680-1876* , 1893.

Johnston, John C. (ed.), *Treasury of the Scottish Covenant* , 1887.

Maclean, Donald, *Aspects of Scottish Church History* , 1927.

M'Crie, Thomas, *Sketches of Scottish Church History* , 2 Vols., 1841 and 1849.

Morrison, George H. (ed.), *Memoirs of the Life, Time, and Writings of the Reverend and Learned Thomas Boston, A. M.,* 1899.

National Covenant of Scotland, The, 1638; (included in many editions of the *Westminster Standards*).

Reformation Principles Exhibited by the Reformed Presbyterian Church in the United States of America, 1919.

Smellie, Alexander, *Men of the Covenant,* 1903, 1909.

Solemn League and Covenant, The, 1643 ; (included in many editions of the *Westminster Standards*).

Spottiswoode, John, *History of the Church of Scotland, 203-1625* , 3 Vols. (Vol. II contains the complete text of the *Second Book of Discipline*); 1851.

Stanley, Arthur Penrhyn, *Lectures on the History of the Church of Scotland, Delivered in Edinburgh in 1872* , 1872.

Summary of the Testimony of the Reformed Presbyterian Church of Scotland, 1932.

Testimony of the Reformed Presbyterian Church of Ireland , 2 Vols., 1912.

Thomson, John H. (ed.), *A Cloud of Witnesses for the Royal Prerogatives of Jesus Christ* , 1871.

Walker, Patrick, *Six Saints of the Covenant* , 2 Vols., 1901.

Wodrow, Robert, *The History of the Sufferings of the Church of Scotland   From the Restoration to the Revolution* , 4 Vols., 1829-1835.

Abjuration Act, 81.
Act of Classes, 63, 68, 69, 224.
Act of Toleration, 164.
Act Rescissory, 79, 80, 141, 155.
Adamson party, 166.
Adamson, Patrick, 29.
"Angelical Assembly", 36.
Apologetical Declaration, 121
Argyle, Marquis of, 83, 128, 194.
Assertory Act, 82.
Associate Presbytery, 165, 203.
Associate Reformed Church (American), 170.
Auchensaugh, 164, 169.
Ayrsmoss, battle of, 106.

Barclay, George, 131.
Beaton David, 182.
Beaton, James, 17, 18.
"Bishops Drag-Net", 86.
Bishops, Tulchan, 28, 29.
"Black Acts", 32, 33.
Blue Banner, 54.
Book of Canons, 25, 39, 40.
Bothwell, battle of, 96, 105.

Cameron, Richard, 100, 105, 116, 118, 123, 216-217.
Cargill, Donald, 110, 118, 130.
Charles I, 46, 48, 49, 50, 53, 54, 58, 61, 62, 64.
Charles II, 64, 65, 66-67, 75, 76, 82, 117, 185.

Chiliasm, 127.
Clarkson, Andrew, 165.
Claverhouse, Graham of, 104.
Conventicles, 86-91.
Cotterel, Colonel, 71.
Court of High Commission, 36, 86.
Cromwell, Oliver, 63, 65, 66, 67, 68, 71-75, 156.
Curates, 86, 142.
Cuthbertson, John, 170, 172.

Dickson, David, 71.
Douglas, Robert, 75.
Drumclog, battle of, 104.
"Drunken Parliament", 79.
Dunbar, battle of, 65, 66.
Dunse Law, encampment at, 54.

Engagement, the, 61-63.
Erastianism, 149-150, 151, 152, 153, 158, 207-213.

"Four Tables", the, 45-46.
Fraser, James, 170, 172.
Free Church of Scotland, 178, 181.

General Assembly of 1638, 51-53.
Gib, John, 130.
Gillespie, George, 59, 201.
Gillespie, Patrick, 68, 73.
Glass, John, 202.

Grant party, 168.
Grant, Patrick, 167.
Gray, Robert, 108.
"Great Charter of Presbytery", 32-33, 55.
Guthrie, James, 56, 57, 68, 194.
Guthrie, John, 194.
Guthrie, William, 123.

Hall, Henry, 110.
Hall, James, 172, 173, 175.
Hamilton Declaration (1679), 108-110
Hamilton, Marquis of, 49.
Hamilton, Patrick, 17, 18.
Hamilton, Robert, 163, 164.
Harleyites, 167.
Harleys, Andrew, 167.
Harleys, John, 167.
Harlite party, 167.
Henderson, Alexander, 47, 48, 52, 185.
Houston, David, 159.
Howdenites, 167.

Indulgences, 91-101.
Informatory Vindication, 131.

James VII, 90, 91, 97-98, 100-101, 138.

Kid, John, 100.
Knox, John, 19-24, 28-29, 207.

Lanark Declaration, 119-120.
Laud, Archbishop, 39, 46.
Leighton, Robert, 94.
Leslie, General, 54, 66.
Liturgy, controversy about, 41-44.

Mackenzie, Sir George, 126.
Macmillan, John, 159-165, 167, 169.
Macneill, John, 165.
Mair, Thomas, 167, 170.
Melville, Andrew, 29-32, 35.
Melville, James, 29.
Middleton, Earl of, 77.

Nairne, Thomas, 168, 169, 172, 204.
Naseby, battle of, 65.
National Covenant (1580), 185.
National Covenant (1638), 48-49, 81, 83, 185, 187-188.

Peden, Alexander, 124, 132.
Pentland rising 102-103.
Perth, Five Articles of, 38-39.
Ploughlandhead Testimony, 147-153, 175.
Preston, battle of, 63.
Public Resolutions, the, 68.
Queensferry Paper, the, 110-116, 118, 224.
Reformed Presbytery (First American), 170.

Reformed Presbytery of Edinburgh, 173-174.
Reformed Presbytery (Scotland), 169, 170, 171-173.
Renwick, James, 100, 127, 131-132.
Resolutioners and Protestors, 68-71, 85.
Revolution of 1688, 138.
Revolution Settlement, 138-158.
Rullion Green, battle of, 102-103.
Russel, James, 130-131.
Rutherford, Samuel, 58, 68, 194, 201, 215,.
Rutherglen Testimony, 110, 107.

Sanquhar Declaration, 105, 116-118, 224.
Second Book of Discipline , 211-212.
Sharp, James, 75, 103.
Shields, Alexander, 84, 125, 143, 144, 145, 217.
Shields, Michael, 134.
Smith, Walter, 135.
Smoking Flax, 168.
Solemn League and Covenant, 55-58, 83, 185, 188-193.
Spottiswoode, 37, 38.
"Sweet Singers", the, 130.
"Tender", the, 67.
"Test", the, 82, 83.

Test Act, 118.
Turner, Sir James, 101.

United Original Secession Church, 205.
United Presbyterian Church of North America, 170.
United Societies, the, 161-165.

Walker, Patrick, 95, 98, 99, 100, 126, 163-164, 201.
Wallace, Colonel James, 102.
Wariston, Johnston of, 47, 59, 68.
Welwood, John, 88.
Westminster Assembly, 100.
William of Orange, 138-139.
Wishart, George, 19.
Worcester, battle of, 66.